Surviving Little League

Surviving Little League

For Players, Parents, and Coaches

Les Edgerton
Mike Edgerton

TAYLOR TRADE PUBLISHING
Lanham • New York • Dallas • Toronto • Oxford

Published by Taylor Trade Publishing
An imprint of The Rowman & Littlefield Publishing Group, Inc.
4501 Forbes Boulevard, Suite 200
Lanham, Maryland 20706

Distributed by National Book Network

Library of Congress Cataloging-in-Publication Data

Edgerton, Leslie.
    Surviving Little League : for players, parents, and coaches / Les Edgerton and Mike Edgerton.
        p. cm.
    Summary: A humorous look at the experiences and people connected with Little League baseball.
    ISBN 1-58979-067-7
    1. Baseball—Juvenile literature. 2. Little League baseball—Juvenile literature. [1. Little League baseball—Humor. 2. Baseball—Humor.] I. Edgerton, Mike, 1989– II. Title.
    GV867.5 .E37 2004
    796.357'62—dc22   2003018267

♾™ The paper used in this publication meets the minimum requirements of American National Standard for Information Sciences—Permanence of Paper for Printed Library Materials, ANSI/NISO Z39.48–1992.
Manufactured in the United States of America.

For my beautiful wife and Mike's mom Mary—"Missus Coach"—who is the love of both of our lives and who wasn't a baseball fan until her husband and son became involved, but is now our biggest booster. When Mike's at bat he can always pick Mom's voice out above all the other parents in the stands when she cuts loose with her favorite cheer of encouragement for her baby boy to, "Pick one out and give it a ride!" What's great about Mary is that she never knows the final score of any of his games and could care less, but her first question to Mike is always, "Did you have a good time?" Mary wasn't much of a fan of any sport when we got married—in fact, during our first years of marriage a local TV news-sports-and-weather program posed a nightly "Sports Trivia" question to viewers to which her stock answer was invariably the one athlete whose name she was familiar with: "Lew Alcindor" (which meant that about once a year she nailed the correct response). She didn't know much about baseball when our hardball odyssey began when Mike was five, but at this point, after she's viewed several hundred of Mike's games, I wouldn't want her in my Fantasy Baseball League unless I was content to settle for second place. She wouldn't have time anyway; she's starring in another "fantasy" league that's mine alone. . . .

Mike and I both want to also dedicate this book to every one of the boys and girls involved in youth baseball. Our wish for each one of you is that "the wind be blowing in when you're pitching . . . and blowing out when you're hitting."

"Let's play two!" —Famous quote from Cub Ernie Banks

CONTENTS

ACKNOWLEDGMENT

With much gratitude to Jill Langford, who saw this as a book that might make a difference in the way young boys and girls are treated in youth baseball.

The Big Lie(s)

1

INTRODUCTION

Greetings to all you boys and girls who own a baseball glove and/or an aluminum Louisville Slugger. This is a book intended for you—the young baseball player. Please try to keep it hidden from your parents, coaches, and other adults—you know, those large people with thinning hair and bulging stomachs and really bad breath. They haven't yet developed the keen sense of humor you possess and may take offense at some of the concepts included here. And you know from experience what it means when adults get mad at you—no Nintendo 64 or Sony Playstation for a week! Prison time in your room. Sometimes, they even take away your allowance! (A hint: Don't hide this book under your mattress. That's the first place they look.)

There are a few things you should know when you decide to go out for a youth baseball team. This book outlines some of the trials and tribulations you'll face during your baseball-playing years. It also provides some strategies for overcoming the weird decisions made on your behalf by those large people in charge of your lives who will tell you what they are doing is "for your own good" or "for the good of the team."

(I'll tell you a secret—I'm much older than you and I still get a sinking feeling in my stomach when someone tells me they're about to do something "for my own good." Some things never change.)

If you haven't figured it out yet, let me tell you that some of the adults you'll meet during your baseball career aren't the brightest people in the world (which may be why they're coaching youth baseball and not sitting in the dugout at Wrigley Field). Although . . . some are. Smart, I mean—not the Wrigley Field thing. Some coaches are really intelligent and know the game and you can even be friends with them. I, of course, was one such coach. I could have even been in the Wrigley Field dugout, but chose coaching younger players instead. The only thing that kept me from the ivied walls of Wrigley or from having the Green Wall of Fenway as my office view was . . . I was a lousy ballplayer when I was a kid. A right fielder. If you could have seen me trying to catch a fly ball, you would have doubled over in hysterical laughter.

Along the way, besides dispensing some really useful advice for you on how to get the most out of your baseball experience and maybe even have some of that elusive "fun" adults are always yapping about that they insist you're going to have playing ball, I'll expose some myths you may have heard about our national pastime.

For instance, how many times have you had a coach or parent get down on one knee, look you square in the eye with the seriousness of a politician, and say, "There's no *I* in *Team*"?

What a crock!

I like former N.Y. Yankee superstar Reggie Jackson's reply to that one, when he told the coach who said that to him: "There might not be any *I* in '*Team*'... but there is in '*Win*'."

Do you know what the biggest lie told in America is? My intensive research clearly establishes that the single largest falsehood uttered in this country is: "Son, I was a shortstop when I played."

Yeah.

If that was true, judging by the vast numbers of adults who make that claim—coaches and dads, primarily—then the following conclusions could be accurately made:

1. *If you have aspirations to coach after your playing days are over, unless you were a shortstop, lose that ambition.* Players who've played other positions just aren't allowed to coach when they reach the legal voting age. It seems to be an unwritten law. If you played right field, for instance, forgive me while I laugh uncontrollably when you tell me you want to coach when you get bigger. In seven years of coaching youth baseball, I've never heard another coach besides myself admit to playing right field.

2. *Based on the vast numbers of adults who claimed to have been a shortstop, it's logical to assume that most teams "in the day" lined up all nine defensive players between second and third.* That must have looked weird! *Nobody* played the outfield! That is, if you buy the claims of most coaches and some dads. Oh, I forgot. Besides shortstop, an adult may sometimes claim they were a pitcher or even a catcher. Once in a while, they may even say they played another infield position. But, *no one* in youth coaching ever claims to have played the outfield. At least not right field.

3. *There is only one position worth playing, and that is shortstop.* If that's the only position older folks claim to have played, then all the other positions (with the exception of pitcher and maybe catcher) must be dog doo-doo. Being a pitcher is cool, and there are some who will tell you they were their team's hurler, but be suspicious when you ask them to show you how to throw a curve and they claim they can't, as they "threw out their arm" years ago and don't want to risk further injury. After all, when you're now a successful accountant, throwing out your arm can ruin your business career (that's your adding machine arm!) and one can't be too careful. Claiming to have been a catcher is also somewhat cool, as that gives the adult the opportunity to tell you how "tough" a player must be to squat down behind the plate, implying that even though they missed being in the Marine party that landed on Iwo Jima by an unlucky birth date, they are just as tough and rugged as those heroes because they blocked pitches in the dirt. (Or tried to. Unless the catchers in your coach's time were infinitely better than the ones of today, more balls skidded to the backstop than were blocked, I suspect.)

The truth. . . .

The truth is, most of your coaches and dads probably played the outfield, and I have a suspicion many of them played the dreaded right field. Just like today, the rule existed that all players have to be given an inning in the infield during the game. What probably was your coach's "real" experience was that in a blow-out and in a late inning, his coach put him on third or second base and closed his eyes, hoping he wouldn't make too many errors and let the other team back into the game. Playing that one inning on third, they were "close" to short and it doesn't really take that much of a stretch of the imagination to slide a few steps over (in their somewhat fuzzy memory) and find themselves covering the "hole." Or maybe they even did play short for an inning or two. Who knows? I'm even fairly positive that some of those who claim to have played the "6" spot in their team's lineup really did. I just don't think I've met them. I've always wished that when a coach claimed to have been a shortstop he could be required to take a lie detector test.

I think what would happen in that event is that most "former shortstops" would decline because the electrodes they hook up to your arm might short-circuit and shock them and that would be a calamity in their present job—you know, that, "I don't want to risk further injury. . . ." After all, when you're now a successful accountant, electrocuting your arm can ruin your calculator mechanics and one can't be too careful.

Here's another one you may have been told. "Son, I always batted third (or fourth) for my team."

Excuse me?

If those claims are to be believed, judging from the vast numbers of coaches who make that claim, the only way that could be true is if their team's lineup had read thusly:

Batting Order for the
Gobbler's Knob Mauling Marauders:

1. Jimmy Swarsky
2. Sandy Smith
3A. Dennis Jones
3B. Nancy Ebersole
3C. Randy Higgins
3D. "Pee Wee" Johnson
3E. Dusty Palmer
3F. Mike Lentil
3G. Randy Rangoon
3H. Percy Saunders
3I. **(Your Coach's name here)**
3J. Milton Ebersole

Provided their coach filled out their batting order as per the above, what they're telling you is probably true.

I'd still be skeptical.

Call me cynical, but I suspect he batted in the "3J" spot. . . .

The third big lie you're apt to hear is, "I just want to make this season fun for the kids. I don't care if we win or not just as long as all the kids have fun." This statement will come from a large, older person who will insist you call him "Coach."

Don't take what he says literally. There's a good chance that his idea of "fun" is probably going to be somewhat different than yours.

This book came about because one day a couple of years ago, my then-eleven-year-old son Mike had just had a rather devastating experience on his Little League team. It wasn't his first bad experience—just the most recent. His coach had told him a few days before that he would be the starting pitcher in the next game . . . and then changed his mind at the last second and had his own son start. This was fairly typical behavior for this coach, and Mike took it stoically, but I could tell it hurt him. Back at my computer, I started thinking about this guy and began writing a tongue-in-cheek description of him and his actions as coach. Mike wandered back and began reading it. And laughing.

"Dad," he said, "this is really good—makes me feel better." He suddenly wrinkled up his brow—a "sign"

I recognized as brain activity going on inside his noggin—and he looked up at me and said, "I've got an idea. Why don't you and I write a book about all the kinds of bad coaches there are in baseball? You know, the ones who dump on kids."

I saw what a great idea that was instantly. The best part of Mike's idea was that we write it together. Which we ended up doing. Most of the "types" depicted in this book were proposed by Mike, along with most of the details that delineated them. Not to mention that he furnished a ton of the descriptions and anecdotes and lots of the other stuff you'll find in here. The most important thing Mike brought to our writing table, however, was his particular sensibility as a kid who'd been through the Little League baseball wars—a sensibility I wouldn't have been able to capture without his help. This is a truly collaborative effort and probably the most fun I've ever had with my buddy, Mike.

What I think makes our effort even more credible is that Mike happens to be one of those kids who's had a large share of success in youth baseball. He's not a kid who's speaking from a reservoir of bitterness. Sure, he's had his share of unfair treatment from coaches and others in youth baseball, but he's also had a lot of good things happen, too. When he was in Little League, he was a perennial All-Star, and when he left Little League a couple of years ago, he first played on an AABC team and then went on to play for the Indy

Bandits, a select team that plays in the Southwest Ohio League, one of the premier youth baseball leagues in the country. This year, he returned to Ft. Wayne to "play up" for a fourteen-year-old team, the Frozen Ropes (he's thirteen). Both teams the past two years qualified to play in the NBC (Bandits) and USTOC (Ropes) World Series. Unfortunately, Mike broke two toes the day the Frozen Ropes learned they were going to Joplin and he was unable to play.

The thing is, even though Mike has been blessed in having four of the five "tools" in baseball (alas, he has no "wheels"—most turtles could spot him ten yards and still win a 100-yard race), he's also always been aware when teammates haven't been treated fairly or have had a bad experience, and he's always tried to do something to help them over the rough spots—by extending a helping hand, listening with a sympathetic ear, or asking me what he could do to help the player. He saw this book as a way for those kids who have bad experiences to get the last laugh.

I agree.

Hope you do, too.

The Kinds of Coaches You're Likely to Encounter and How to Deal with Them

ll kinds.

But most will fall into one of the several categories you'll find in the following chapters in this section.

THE BLUSTERER

Also called the "Marine sergeant." This is usually a big guy. Big from east-to-west, that is. (You know—a "wide body.") Height-wise, he probably towers over most of the kids by an inch or two. Maybe not. The Blusterer also comes in other body types, so don't be quick to assume the tall, skinny guy isn't one of this breed. Or, the short stumpy dude. Mostly though, they're built like Bluto and have thick, bristly eyebrows that are connected to each other. They never let their hair get longer than 3/4 of an inch. They were never actually in the Marines—or any other branch of the service—but they imagine how it was. Their knowledge of military matters is mostly gleaned from movies starring actors who also weren't in the service.

Even bigger than this guy's girth is his voice. You can hear him clear out in right field, even if you're up against the fence. And that's when he's whispering.

This kind of coach is a freak on "conditioning." "Laps" is his middle name. No, make that his *first* name! You boot a ground ball and you'll find yourself jogging around the outfield. Or hear him scream to "drop and give me ten." Don't you just love this guy? He's dedicated the first hour of practice to Olympic warm-ups and the Special Forces's exercise regimen. You'll notice he never takes part in these fun activities. Can you imagine him doing a sit-up? (Okay—I'll wait a minute here until you can control your giggling. . . .)

At his evolutionary height, the Blusterer has the firm opinion that, after an hour and a half of wind sprints, only a wuss would dare request a sip of water. "No pain, no gain" is his mantra. He thinks nine-year-old kids are soft beyond belief and it is up to him to do his part to get you ready for the invasion by the Commies that's coming. He has a million stories about how rough he had it as a kid and how kids today don't have any guts. He was also probably unbelievably poor as a kid (according to him). He'll have a story or two to illustrate that. Like, "When I was a kid, we were soooo poor . . . that my dad would give us eleven kids a quarter to skip supper." (Typically, watery gruel and a piece of day-old bread . . . the heel. All eleven kids got the heel.) "Then, while we were sleeping, he'd sneak into our (communal) bedroom and steal the quarter from under our pillows where we were told to put it . . . and in the morning, punish us for losing the quarter by taking away our breakfasts."

Dude! This was some tough, poor kid! It's no wonder he sees all of you as soft. (Hint: Give him a quarter and maybe he'll take it easy on you. Just don't tell him to hide it under his pillow or he'll become suspicious.)

He may actually have been in the Marines, and if so, he'll tell you all about it. (All except the part where he was a clerk-typist and stationed in Kokomo, Indiana.)

He hates players who look like miniature versions of himself. If you're a bit overweight, run like the wind from this guy! Join the chess club instead and learn how to do that castle move thingamajig. His mission, as he sees it, is to make you all combat-ready. He has a poster of Bobby Knight in his bedroom and he can quote long passages from Vince Lombardi. His wife calls him "Sir." He thinks Woody Hayes got a raw deal for slugging one of his football players and losing his job. He thinks Ty Cobb was misunderstood when he tried to decapitate the second baseman with his spikes.

He especially likes coaching baserunning, particularly the fine art of sliding into a player and aiming your spikes at the fielder's groin. He'll show you how to use an emery board to "sharpen" your rubber spikes. He goes around muttering, "If you ain't bleeding, you ain't hurt. Get up, you sissy. That arm ain't broke bad. I don't see no stinkin' bone stickin' out."

He'll tell you he was a power-hitting third baseman, but you are convinced secretly that the only sport he could have been good at would have been sumo wrestling.

How do you deal with this guy?

Easy.

Be his son.

Well . . . actually, it's not all that easy being his son. Prepare for a lot of practice and "acting like a man." (A nine-year-old "man.")

If you can't arrange that, the next best alternative is to perfect the art of invisibility. Try to blend into the background. When the team's all gathered around for his words of wisdom and carnage, arrange to be hidden in the middle of the other players, preferably near the back. Crouch down a bit so he can't see you.

If that doesn't work, try the other tack. He likes loud kids, so be vocal. Show him you're competitive. If you're playing in the infield and the second baseman boots a grounder, snarl at the offender something like, "Yo, pansy! Pretty boy with all your teeth! Get in front of the ball. Do or die! Semper fie!" Try to put nails in your voice. If not nails, broken glass.

When you slide, try to (temporarily) "take out" the fielder covering the base. After the play, stand over the fallen victim and sneer at him (or her) and emit a guttural snarl. If your sneer isn't that great, get in front of a mirror at night and practice, practice, practice!

At the conclusion of the exercise portion of your practice (that hour and a half deal), if he lets the team take a water break (doubtful, but if he does, here's your chance), speak up loudly so all can hear, "Only punks need water. Sure are a lot of punks on this here team." He'll love this and probably make you the shortstop and it's for sure you're going to bat cleanup and be made team captain.

In other words, do everything in your power to become a bully. Cultivate obnoxious traits to the best of your ability. Your purpose in life on his team is not to win friends, but games. He relates to this and you'll become his best friend. He may even want to adopt you! (Failing that, you may be lucky enough to be invited over to his house where he will teach you how to field-strip an M-1 blindfolded in less than thirty-two seconds, a valuable skill you'll be glad you learned when those nasty Commies finally invade our shores and you can be sure they will.)

When you're at bat and swing at a pitch that's over your head, he knows you're not wearing your glasses and therefore didn't realize your mistake and will so inform you: "That pitch was a mile over your head, you dummy!" he'll scream, and spit out his sunflower seeds. The best thing for you to do at that point is turn toward him, stand at ramrod-straight attention, and yell back, *"Sir! Yessir!* I know I messed up! *Sir!"* This will touch the soft spot in his heart and he'll forgive you. When you get back to the dugout, be sure to let him know you've committed the very worst of all the possible Seven Deadly Baseball Sins—swinging at a high pitch—and that you fully expect retribution in the

afterlife unless somehow he finds it in his heart to forgive you.

In case you don't know, these are the Seven Deadly
Baseball Sins in this man's lights:

1. Swinging at a high pitch
2. Not hustling
3. Not hustling
4. Not hustling
5. Not hustling
6. Not hustling
7. Drinking water

You'll notice numbers two through six appear to be
very similar. Perhaps so, but there are very important
subtle differences in each. Sin number two, for instance,
involves not crashing into a fence while chasing a foul
pop fly. If you do (crash into the fence), and don't draw
blood or at least break a minor bone, you have still
erred grievously. Sin number six means you failed to
inflict damage on the catcher when sliding into home
plate. The purpose of sliding into home is to cause the
opponent's catcher to yank off his equipment and make
a request to his coach to play right field from this point
hence. If he doesn't do that, you've failed in your mission and are guilty of a heinous crime.

There are a few more signs that will tell you when
you've been lucky enough to have drawn The Blusterer,
but I think those I've given you will be enough to help
you make that assumption.

If you feel you can't carry out the suggestions I've given you for dealing with this character, then your best course of action is to get padding for every part of your body and cleverly hide it with your uniform. And get your folks to buy you a thin water bottle, one you can hide on your person where the coach can't see it. From time to time, pretend you're puking and walk over to the side, turn your back to the coach, and make retching noises. This will gain you lots of points with this man. Sneak a sip or two between retches. If he catches you drinking from your secret source, his reaction to that will probably cause a bit of panic in you. In that event, try your best to remember this number:

9-1-1.

Good luck!

CHAPTER
TWO

THE "EXPERT"

Here's the second type of coach you may encounter:

This guy is Mr. Baseball. He knows ten times more than Bob Uecker ever hoped to know about the game. He has a library of over 102 baseball books. He also has all the Tom Emanski videos as well as nineteen others from various sources, even one narrated in Japanese and featuring shorter players!

His practice time is mostly spent in strategy sessions with the team gathered on the grass around him. Kind of like Aristotle at the Forum (or wherever Mr. A did his thing). He'll be giving you problems such as: "When there are two outs, the score is tied, we've got a pitcher on the mound with a good fastball, a so-so change-up, and a nasty curve; the other team has runners on first and third, but the runner on third is slow; the batter has a 2-2 count and has just fouled off eleven pitches in a row, seven to the left foul line, three to the right, and one straight back; my question to you boys is: where should the right fielder position himself, what pitch should the pitcher throw, and who really stole the Lindbergh baby?"

Yo, coach. You said *question*. That's *questionz*— plural. I forgot my calculator, Coach Professor. Anybody here got a pencil and piece of scrap paper? Give me a minute; I'll figure it out. On second thought, give me *two* minutes, please. Remember, I'm only ten and in the middle third of my class and I'm at a really bad school according to my parents.

That's an example of what *not* to say. It's okay to think it. Just don't say it.

What this coach is after is a wrong answer. His objective is to show all you guys (and girls) how much he knows. Don't spoil it for him. Give him what he wants: a wrong answer. Throw out anything you like, the dumber the better. That way he can shine and draw your oohs and aahs of admiration for his baseball intellect. Cross him and give him the correct answer and prepare to bear the wrath of Ghengis Khan. Pencil yourself in as the *substitute* right fielder. You'll be batting last.

Give him the wrong answer and let him do his thing and you can run to your parents after practice with glee in your step and excitement in your voice as you announce you're the starting shortstop and will be batting third in the next game.

Remember this man's situation in life and you'll know why he's like this. He's the third-shift maintenance guy down at the ice cream factory and he has a master's degree in biochemistry. His problem, which he'll tell you about if you ask—and maybe even if you don't—is that every job he's applied for he's been turned down as being "overqualified." Or, (he won't tell you this, but it's probably true) if he ever had gotten a decent job, he was fired within a month for "lacking social skills" or even as a "borderline sociopath with garrulous tendencies." Plus, tending the boiler and making sure no one breaks in to steal a gallon or two of Chocolate Ripple Delight from his employer, the Big Globule Ice Cream Company, enables him to pursue his real passions—writing unrhymed poetry, reading sci-fi books, and pondering the meaning of the universe, having already discovered it centered around him. He is one small step removed from being a fanatic—the definition of a fanatic being a person who does what God would do if God had all the facts. . . . He doesn't relate well to other adults, but some kids are fooled by him and they form his primary circle of admirers.

The best way to deal with this kind of coach? Always take a book with you to practice and make sure he sees you reading it on breaks. A good one to carry is anything by Ayn Rand. If you don't care for Ms. Rand's prose (or know who she is), get one of her books anyway, hollow it out, and stick in your favorite R. L. Stein or Matt Christopher novel.

And water breaks can be fun with this guy—much more so than with The Blusterer. Engage him in a discussion about whether there has ever been life on Mars or how many unassisted triple plays there have been in major league history, and your entire practice can consist of one water break! You'll be logy from the H_2O you've consumed by the time your parents arrive! Before you run to the car, however, wait to get the nine-page handout he's prepared for you, outlining the subtle positioning of the center fielder on "wheels" plays.

And be thankful. You could have gotten The Blusterer!

CHAPTER
THREE

MANAGER–DAD

The next kind of coach you may get is the father of one of your teammates.

You know this guy. The only reason he's coaching is so his own boy can play shortstop and pitch. On another team, coached by another coach, his son is destined for right field. He can't play the "6" spot on that team . . . because *that* coach's son is playing shortstop when he's not on the mound.

Realistically, it's going to be hard *not* to get this coach, as that's why 102.3 percent of youth coaches are coaching—to watch out for their own son and be sure he gets the prime position. More than likely, you'll get a coach who has a son on the team at least four times in your career. That is, if you end up playing four years. If you play five years, you'll probably get five of these guys. Six years, six such coaches. Seven . . . hey . . . *you* do the math. This type will usually also have traits of one of the other types as well, i.e., The Blusterer, The Expert, etc.

The best way to deal with this guy?

Easy.

Same way you would with The Blusterer.

Be his son.

If you can't arrange that, simply mentally cross yourself off the short list for shortstop and/or pitcher (or aim to be the backup short or the second or third pitcher), and make it your more realistic goal to be the first, second, or third baseman. Or catcher.

You'll probably end up in right field anyway, but it's nice to dream.

A really good strategy if you get this coach is to become best friends with his son. See if you can get invited to an overnight at his house. Do that, and you're in. Bond with the kid's dad—call him "Coach" a lot and put the capital in it when you say it, reverently and with a bit of awe in your voice. Ask him if anyone has ever really shined those Florsheims you see over in the corner the right way and tell him that you'd like to buff 'em up for him if he'd allow you to. Arrange to have your shoeshine rag with you and spit on it with panache as you make your request.

Ask him to help you out with your playing. Tell him it's your dream to play first and maybe pitch a little. Be sure you get it across somehow that you would never consider yourself in the same league as his own son, but that you highly admire his boy's skills and want to be just like him (his son) when you grow up. Say that even if his son is a year younger than you. "When you grow up" is just a saying. Tell him that you and his boy have been practicing together a lot and that if he put you on first base, you think you can handle his little puny lob throws over to first better than anyone on the team. Only, don't say, "little puny lob throws." Instead, use the term, "highly accurate bullet tosses." Inform him that as a first baseman, you appreciate accuracy way more than speed. Tell him you don't mind a bit that the throw from deep short bounces eight times on average and is wide right when his son makes the heave. On second thought, forget that last. He may misinterpret what you're saying.

If you do all this and still see yourself heading for right field, there's one last thing you might try. Ask him if he'll adopt you. It may not work, but what the heck—you were headed for right field anyway. It's worth a try.

First base is kind of cool, by the way.

CHAPTER
FOUR

COACH "STEREOTYPE"

Enter the next coaching type—Coach Stereotype.

This guy's a gem. He knows every cliché in baseball. That's not the problem. The problem is . . . he believes them.

This is the guy who thinks second basemen should be little wiry guys and fast runners. Hustle guys. Doesn't matter if they couldn't catch a grounder with a ten-foot glove. If you're little, wiry, and can run a sub four-minute mile, you're going to be the second baseman, count on it.

Wilbur Wood would never have pitched for this guy. In case you haven't heard of Wilbur Wood, he was an

All-Star pitcher for the Chicago White Sox back in the day. He didn't fit the pitcher stereotype, being a bit portly and not the fastest or most svelte guy in baseball. Kind of a David Wells type—if you know what I mean—for a more contemporary example.

This is a gentleman who makes his fielding assignments based on style. If you're flashy and look good in your uniform, you're the shortstop. Especially if you're good at making "alibi dives" after ground balls twenty feet to your left that you couldn't possibly reach even if you had forty-five minutes to get there. If you're smart, you'll even dive for balls hit to the opposite side of wherever you're playing. If you're playing shortstop, for instance, leap at everything hit to the first baseman. Get lots of dirt on your uniform and flop to the ground every chance you get. To this coach, this indicates "hustle" and he absolutely loves hustle, both the pretend kind and the sincere kind. They are both the same in his mind.

He has a profile firmly established in his mind for how the player for each position should look. Babe Ruth would have been on the bench on this guy's team.

My wife, Mary (Missus Coach), has a term she's coined about certain kids. She calls them "overlooked kids." What she means is kids who don't carry themselves noticeably or with flair. They kind of disappear when around other kids. In other words, their style of comporting themselves doesn't make them stand out. That describes an awful lot of kids, unfortunately. They're always being judged on appearances and it takes a smart adult to disregard that and look at their accomplishments instead.

Alas, Coach Stereotype isn't one of those smart adults. He looks at a boy or girl and instantly makes a judgment about their baseball ability based on the way they look to him.

That energetic chatterbox who's always running everywhere is the guy he likes. It helps to have your uniform tailored by an expert tailor if you want to get on this guy's good side. Make sure your hat looks cool—get one of those stretching kits they sell in the cap shop at the mall. Wear a good uniform and look sharp in it, and it won't matter if you can catch a ground ball or not as long as you can make the miss or error look close. Try to catch at least one out of every seven or eight balls hit to you. As long as you look like "Charley Hustle" it won't matter if you don't catch most of them. It'll help your cause if you walk around muttering, "They oughta let that Pete Rose guy into the Hall of Fame" a lot, especially in his presence. Do a lot of "alibi dives." If, on the other hand, you happen to be one of those "overlooked kids" who makes play after play like a machine but has the physique of a Babe Ruth, you'll probably find yourself making those plays in right field. No matter what you do, you're probably doomed to that position. Blame the diet your folks forced you to follow.

You can move up in the batting order with this guy, however. All you have to do is bat .750 and you'll eventually be moved to the seventh spot. Hey, that's better than where he had you originally, at the twelfth hole, isn't it? Hit five or six home runs in a couple of games and you may even get as high as sixth in the order. Don't expect much more than that.

If you can, talk your parents into modeling classes. They will teach you the kind of grace and posture this guy admires. Don't waste your folks' money on batting or fielding lessons and such. Don't squander your time on playing ball in the backyard with your dad or friends to get better, either. Those skills don't push his buttons that much. The key to this guy is, look good and you'll do good.

Here's the position you'll get from this guy, based on your body type and other qualities.

Tall, left-handed: You're the first baseman. Or maybe the left fielder, if there are two of you who are tall and left-handed. The one who is more left-handed will be the first baseman.

Short, chubby: Congratulations! You're the team's catcher.

Slim, stylish, flashy, with the Derek Jeter look: *Super* congratulations! You're the team's No. 1 pitcher and shortstop! It doesn't matter a bit that your dad's also the coach. (Hint: Get a subscription to *GQ Magazine* and observe how the models carry themselves. When you're in the dugout, try to strike one of their poses.)

Medium build, with front teeth missing and a reputation for hitting other kids all the time while standing in drill lines: You are now the third baseman.

Little, wiry, fast: You already know where you're heading when you take the field. Second base is your home.

All the rest: Outfielders. You're destined to become the next generation of youth coaches. That's the neat thing about being an outfielder. In your adult life, you'll get to reinvent your past and become that shortstop/pitcher you should have been. By then, you will have learned how to be Coach Stereotype yourself. If you haven't learned that, don't expect to coach.

THE "I JUST WANT THE KIDS TO HAVE FUN" COACH; OR, AS HE IS ALSO SOMETIMES KNOWN, "THE MR. ROGERS OF THE DIAMOND"

The next type of coach up to bat is this dude.

This is the guy who called the parents' and players' meeting the second he found out who would be on his team. At the meeting, while you players fidgeted and idly wondered what you'd done in your past life to deserve this, he gave an impassioned, soulful, almost teary-eyed speech (lasting about an hour and ten minutes) on how much he loves kids and how he was going to make sure, above all else, that the players on his team, by cracky, were just going to "have fun."

Precise details on how you were going to have all this "fun" were left a bit unclear. You seem to remember him saying something about all the kids having equal playing time and getting to play all the positions, even the neat ones and even if they weren't very good players.

That was probably about the time you began tuning him out. You most likely turned to the teammate sitting next to you who hadn't heard a word the coach had said (preferring to perfect his armpit-flatulence technique instead) and asked, "Correct me if I'm wrong, but haven't you heard this before somewhere?"

Yes, by golly, my boys are going to have tons of fun even if we don't win a single blessed game, this guy insists. Excuse me, but how much "fun" is realistically possible in a 0-16 season in which you've been ten-run-ruled by the fourth inning in twelve of those contests?

Of course, he neglects to explain how that happens.

The reason is he doesn't expect that to happen.

Only it will.

He also doesn't stop to think about what he's doing when he inserts little "Jiminy Cricket" Sanders (not his real name) at the "hot corner" despite little Jiminy being terrified beyond all reasonable fear that a ball will be hit to him during his sentence there. And, of course, such a ball will be hit to him. A screamer. By "Muscles" Malone, the 6-foot, 3-inch behemoth on the Sandusky Gravediggers, your first opponent. Opposing coaches always check Muscles's driver's license to make sure he really is the eleven years of age he claims to be. Your center fielder will tell you later he could hear the ball whistling as it left Muscles's bat . . . headed to . . . you guessed it. Third base and little Jiminy C.

The whole team should show up at little Jiminy's funeral. It's only proper. . . .

How to survive a coach like this?

Don't be the coach's son.

Your family will end up in poverty when little Jiminy's parents sue your dad.

If you can't arrange that (not being the coach's son) then you might try talking in tongues and handling live rattlesnakes and telling everyone you meet that someone is whispering to you in your head and telling you to get Dad's chain saw and cut down all houses painted blue. This kind of behavior will (hopefully) get you committed to an insane asylum—then you won't have to go through the years of poverty ahead of you because of your dad's coaching and the subsequent lawsuits. Life in the asylum isn't the greatest, but at least you'll have three square meals a day and won't be forced to play all nine positions, sometimes in a single game. Sometimes in a single inning. . . .

If, on the other hand, you are singularly blessed and *aren't* this coach's son, what can you do to survive a season under him?

Read every baseball book you can get your hands on so you'll at least know the basics of each position. This knowledge may save your life. Late at night, when your folks are sleeping, sneak downstairs, pop in baseball instructional videos, and watch them until your eyeballs bleed and your grades all go to Fs. This is *survival*, buddy, and it's more important that you get through the season without anything much worse than a broken bone or two than keep up your schoolwork. After all, what good is getting into Harvard if you're in a permanent full body cast? Or suffering from a permanent nervous tremor due to your experiences under this man? Let's face it—you're not going to become the CEO of IBM if you blink 100 rpms per second and your left arm constantly flies up uncontrollably at inopportune and unforeseen moments and hits you in the nose, now are you? Next year, under a different coach, you can catch up on your schoolwork and still be accepted at a decent college. Maybe not Harvard, or even Yale, but a good, solid school. Arkansas A&M comes to mind. . . .

Kiss Harvard goodbye if you get this coach.

Only . . . it isn't as bad as I make it out to be. This guy isn't going to continue being Mr. Nice Guy. After about the sixth blowout, a mysterious chemical reaction is going to take place in his body and he will change before your very eyes. Whereas before, everyone was treated equally, and every player rotated among the nine positions like a baseball version of musical chairs—what we call the "Horsehide Lazy Susan"—now some players will begin to be treated *more* equally than others.

What that means is that the outstanding player on the team is going to suddenly find himself logging a lot more time at shortstop (when he isn't pitching just about every game). That guy who was always looking in the wrong places for grounders on second is going to have to shift his focus skyward . . . where the fly balls are raining down in right field. Before, during the games, this coach was over on the side of the dugout where the bleachers are, chatting up the parents and being all warm and fuzzy with them. Now, he suddenly begins to hang out on the far side, out of sight and definitely out of the range of any possible mutinous mutterings by moms and dads.

If you're lucky (which means, if you're a really bad player), you can begin to breathe a sigh of relief. Your role is going to change from "Rotating Position Man Doomed to Face Daily Danger and Risk of Facial Feature Realignment at the Hot Corner" to . . . "Bench-Warmer." Don't be disappointed. Now you're safe. You can go back to your regular eight hours of sleep at night and turn all those overdue baseball books back in to the library. The only position you'll have to be familiar with is . . . you guessed it: right field.

If, however, the stars are against you, and this kind of coach holds to his original plan, then if I were you

I'd call a secret meeting of all the players at midnight (except his son, natch) and come to a pact in which you all collectively agree to not show up at the next game. When you get his bewildered phone call later, you can all use the common excuse that you "forgot" the game was today.

Look. I know your parents have taught you to be a responsible human being and honor your commitments, but we're talking about your *life* here, pal. Some of you players who know you're not that hot—tell the others what it's like to have to take your mitt out there to third base and try to pretend you're not shaking in your Nike's when that 6-foot 3-inch laboratory mistake from the other team strides up to the plate with a tree limb in his mitts, the ground shaking under his step.

It's downright scary.

This is how Communism started, you know. In Russia, they made it a law that you had to play third base, no matter how unskilled or unprepared for that assignment you were. That was the end of equal play in that poor country. Soon afterwards, the Tsar was toppled by hordes of players forced to play third base and the other players could breathe a sigh of relief and go back to their best position on the field.

The outfield.

The *safe* outfield.

If none of these tactics work, your last resort is to pretend to be an immigrant from an obscure European country who can't understand English, and no matter where the coach tells you to go, just nod and nod and smile and smile (show lots of teeth—you'll probably still have lots of teeth if you haven't yet been forced to play third base) . . . and then run out to right field. He'll probably move you the first few times —maybe even walk out and guide you back in, his arm warmly and fondly around your trembling shoulders—but if you do it enough times, he'll give up and just leave you there. The only problem with that (none of these tactics are foolproof) is that you may find yourself as part of a large crowd in right field, surrounded by nodding, smiling immigrants from East Bulgaria in baseball uniforms (your equally smart teammates who've also glommed onto this book).

Good luck.

I hope you can survive "equal play." I personally know some who have, so it's not impossible.

THE STATS FREAK, OR "HI-TECH FANATIC"

Our next coaching "type" is a real original-diginal.

With a better education, this guy would have been a CIA researcher drone. He knows everything there is to know about his team. He's the guy who will come up to you before your fourth game and say, "Skippy, my figures show you went to the bathroom six times during the last game and went oh-for-four. In our first game, you only went twice and you hit for the cycle. Cut down on the john time, willya? For the team?"

Of course, if this coach also has The Blusterer's coaching tendencies, you won't have to worry about him charting your bathroom time. Not being allowed any water breaks will sharply curtail that particular activity.

But, you can be sure he'll know everything else you've ever done on the baseball diamond.

And I mean *everything*.

You'll know him when you see him. He's the guy with the Palm Pilot and the Pocket Protector that doesn't work. All his shirts have a washed-out blue stain on the pocket from the six leaking ballpoints he always carries. His first priority at the initial team meeting was to find at least two people who would volunteer to keep the scorebook and arrange a six-hour indoctrination meeting with them to be sure they knew how to keep the kind of stats he needed.

Like the tendencies of his left-handed batters against right-handed pitchers when the count was 1 and 2 and the weather was mildly overcast with a prevailing easterly wind at ten knots. During weekday games.

Important stuff like that.

This guy's most vital team member isn't even on the field. He (or she) is in the stands, frantically scribbling down every single twitch both his players and the opponents make. They are usually so busy compiling information for this coach that they don't dare look up when their own son is at bat. Thank goodness they've got the scorebook to check after the game to see how he did! You'll know this person by their conversations with the other parents. He or she will be the one always asking frantically, "What'd Number Thirteen just do?"

You'll earn your position by the book with this coach. Literally.

How do you get a prime position with him?

This is so easy, I'm blushing with shame at the thought you might give me credit for being slick here.

Talk one of your parents into being one of his scorekeepers.

That's part one of your strategy.

Part two is selling your newly appointed score-keeper mom or dad on the concept of fudging a little on your numbers. Have them slip in an extra base hit or so and you'll begin to move up in the batting order.

That error you made last game? Convince them to give it to that kid with the squeaky voice that only dogs can hear clearly who you don't much like because he's always throwing rocks at you and certain other team-mates. You know—the guy whose major claim to fame is that he can make armpit farts with either pit. He'd look better in right field than you would anyway, right?

The only drawback to this plan is that many of these coaches have total recall. They can tell you what the opponent's pitcher threw to your second-sacker in the fourth inning on his third pitch. If you draw one of these guys, there isn't much you can do. You sure can't implement Plan A! It's for sure he's going to remember that the error made at short that let three runs in was yours and not Petey Johnson's (who was playing third that inning). He'll probably also recall that it wasn't your 500-foot home run, but "Big Butt"

McClursky's that won the game against the Weenie Meanie Tigers and that the best you'd done in that particular game was a pop fly that traveled three feet in the air and was caught by the opponent's catcher, who, even though he was looking behind him at the time and trying to rip his mask off, just happened to have his glove stuck out in a defensive position over his head to protect his noggin, which just happened to be where the ball came down.

Teach your scorekeeper parent to be subtle. Tell 'em not to go overboard. Instead of crediting you with that homer, have them merely take away Dummy Zerkel's bunt he beat out for a single in the fourth and award that to you, instead of the SOL (Strikeout, Looking) you really got. (Give that to Dummy.) If they give you an argument, simply inform them that there are two ends to a pencil and there's a reason for that eraser being there, duh! If they still balk, let them know how Dummy Zerkel told you his dad could whip your dad any day of the week and with his metal hook tied behind his back. That should convince them to do a little creative scorekeeping on your behalf.

If none of this works, ask Mr. Stats Freak if you can have a copy of the team's stats. Go over it with a fine-tooth comb and find something you're a leader in. Next practice, while you're on your water break (this guy gives water breaks unless he also has The Blusterer's tendencies), casually make the observation to him that you've noticed the team's H RSP is a pitiful .043 and that if he moved you up to third in the B.O. with your canny eye you feel it would soon soar to way over .100, being as you know perfectly well that with a runner on second, two outs, a count of 2-2 against a lefty who has a fastball in the 55 mph range and always throws outside in this instance, that the duty of the batter is to hit to the opposite field. In case you don't know, "H RSP" stands for "Hits with Runners in Scoring Position" and "B.O." isn't that smell indicator you might have assumed it was, but stands for "Batting Order." Just use the initials though—he'll know what they mean. He may not move you to third from your current position of batting thirteenth, but he may move you up to the "10" spot.

It's worth a shot.

There isn't much else you can do, except possibly improve your numbers. Keep in mind that this guy may say things like, "There's no 'I' in team," but what he really reveres are individual stats. Forget the team here and when he gives you the bunt sign to move along the runner on first (that would be "Nervous Ned" McCallum, who got hit by the pitch in his at-bat), ignore it and hit away. When he starts to chew you out later in the dugout for ignoring his sign and getting a double, just tell him a piece of dust got in your eye and you misread his belt swipe (his "take" sign) for the "hit away" sign (which is a tug at the earlobe). It's easy to confuse the two. He'll forgive you later that night when he pores over the stats and sees you went one-for-four and got an RBI, instead of your usual oh-for-four.

You'll get that "10" spot in the B.O. And just look what you did for the team's H RSP!

If that doesn't earn you the shortstop position, nothing will.

THE "POSSESSED" COACH

You've met 'im. If you haven't, you will.

He's the guy who lives his life vicariously through what you and your teammates do on the field. His son also plays (why else would he coach?) and he's the one he really lives through. The other players are there mostly to be his son's supporting cast in his season of stardom.

He's the guy with absolutely no accomplishments in his own life, other than the time he was tied for "Third Runner-up in the Eastern Quadrant of Indiana Sales for the Third Week of August, 1997," for his company, the Bohunk Paperclip Manufacturing Company.

If you're ever over to his house (to visit his son, your team's shortstop), you can see the certificate proudly mounted above his mantel. Along with his prize, a gift certificate for a Wendy's medium Frosty, which he never cashed in, preferring to display it in a humble, but tasteful, solid gold frame instead. After all, once you scarf down a Frosty, it's gone forever, but if you keep the certificate, well . . . then you've got something.

This coach wasn't even the right fielder when he played. He was the *substitute* right fielder. Batted last. Sometimes his coach "forgot" when it was his time to bat and sent up the lead-off guy instead. After the game, the coach placated him by secretly buying him a Wendy's Frosty (medium) and telling him he'd never make that mistake again. (Until the next game, but he doesn't mention that.) This explains his perhaps unreasonable esteem for Wendy's free Frosty certificates. . . .

It wasn't his fault. At home, he fielded the tennis ball he threw up against the house flawlessly. Over and over, he pounded the stuffing out of the whiffle ball he hit off the tee, smacking more imaginary home runs that one could ever hope to record in a normal lifetime.

It was just during actual games that he sucked.

He was kind of a "choke artist." Meaning, that when something was on the line, like a real ball game against real opponents, he kind of developed the blind staggers. Instead of those nerves of steel he owned during his backyard practice sessions, in a for-real game, those nerves turned to goops of pink marshmallow, causing his legs to turn to grape jelly while he was standing at the plate. Picture that familiar scene of Clark Kent in the phone booth turning into Superman, but run it backwards on the minicam in your brain. Where the Man of Steel turns into the Wimp Reporter.

All that's changed now—mainly, because he doesn't actually have to take the field and play himself. That's your job.

To be what he never was.

It's okay. You're a kid and that's what kids are supposed to do. Atone for the failings of adults when they were kids. Get used to it and don't give me any crybaby stuff like, "It's not fair!" Of course it's not fair, kid! It's not designed to be. If you want fair, don't play baseball on a youth team. Play the Ken Griffey Jr. game on your Nintendo 64 and don't let anyone else have the other set of controls. That's the only time baseball is going to be "fair," chum. I mean—duh—haven't you learned anything here yet?

There's some more stuff you need to know about this guy if you're going to have a chance of dealing with him. You gotta know this, so pay attention.

First, he's now in his fifties. Ever since he became an adult (about the age of thirty-two, when he moved out of his parents' house for the first time), he's been a keen student of baseball. He's got almost twenty years of graduate study in Horsehide Ergonomics. He avidly follows the fortunes of his favorite baseball team (whoever's in first place currently) and knows how to play every position on the field. Especially shortstop, a position he's always admired (from afar), and pitcher.

(Don't make the mistake of assuming he'll be empathetic toward you if you're the same kind of weenie player he was in his own miserable childhood. He hates himself, and when he sees a mirror image of what he used to be, he'll hate you, too. To him, looking at you is like looking into one of those funhouse mirrors that make your image shorter.)

He's got a selective memory. For the life of him, he can't understand what's so hard about hitting a baseball thrown at only 65 mph. At his adult size of 6 foot 2 inches and weighing a few pounds less than a beached Great White, he simply can't comprehend why you think that a five and a half ounce tightly wound baseball thrown faster than the speed limit in most states is fast. Or can hurt, if it happens to strike one of the softer body parts. Like your head. At his present and considerable size, what looks like an Uzi bullet to you looks like a prepubescent girl softball pitcher's changeup to him.

You can use that to your advantage. When you get a pitcher smoking heat past you, just stand up there and snarl, loud enough for Coach to hear, "That all you got, sissy? My mom throws her changeup harder than that." This will get you points. It shows him you're tough. Something else he's always admired. (From afar.)

It also helps to understand this coach's ambitions. He knows that if he guides his team to an undefeated season, he's going to get a call-up to Yankee Stadium. Scouts in pinstripes are in the stands watching his every move (he presumes). He also knows that there will college and pro scouts on hand watching from the bleachers once the word gets out how great his team is playing. Their aim is to give scholarships or signing bonuses to the great players they observe on his team, i.e., his son, your team's shortstop/pitcher.

That's really what he's all about, why he drives you fanatically to "be the best you can be." In his Walter Mitty mind, he fantasizes that once you achieve your perfect season, the following events will unfold: After your miracle season, he will be selected as the All-Star coach. From that position, utilizing all the genius moves he made that got you an undefeated season, his all-star team mows down other all-star teams, one by one, until he arrives with his players on the red-eye to Cooperstown to play in the Little League World Series. After he wins that (with some [limited] help from his players), and immediately after the press conference, a tall man with a bulge of tobacco twixt his cheek and gum will approach him and beg him to join the coaching staff of the Yankees. Of course, they can't offer him the head job—not right away—but they will offer him the third-base coaching position, and it will only be a matter of time before Joe Torre is in the unemployment line and it's him (Possessed Coach) who is barking out at Roger Clemens "Hold 'em, you slacker! You afraid to come inside or something?"

That's his goal and that's his dream and you'd better be aware of it if you hope to have any chance of having a good season with him.

Your best strategy with this man?

Be his son.

Failing that, try to be his nephew.

If that isn't possible, your only recourse is to adopt the rallying cry of the Chicago Cubs.

"Wait'll next year."

THE "KNUTE ROCKNE" OR "RAH-RAH" COACH

This guy you may even like . . . if you're overly impressionable, that is.

He's a speechmaker. A motivator. He's taken the Dale Carnegie salesmanship course six times. In a row. He's on the waiting list for the seventh.

You'll know him when you meet him at the initial team meeting. He's the guy going around to the parents and introducing himself by clasping their handshake hand in both of his (the official Dale Carnegie handshake) and using their first name in every sentence he utters. He'll do the same to you when it's your turn to meet. Expect to get tired of hearing your name. At

the end of the season, you may want to consider chang-
ing it as you're hearing it in your beddy-bye nightmares,
spoken in a voice similar to Coach's.

Nightmares like: "Johnny, (Assuming your name
is Johnny. If not, substitute your own name in the
appropriate places here.) I know you can do this. Hit a
home run to win the game for us, Johnny. Johnny, I
know it's the bottom of the ninth and you haven't had a
hit all year, but Johnny, you can do it! I have faith in you,
Johnny. Your team has faith in you, Johnny. Dale Carnegie
has faith in you, Johnny. Your as-yet-undetermined-and-
future-wife has faith in you, Johnny. Some day, Johnny,
you'll be as old as I am and married and have a kid
(Johnny, Junior) and you'll be telling him about the day
you won the game for the Bellicose Builders, Inc. Little
Scrappers Little League team with a home run one day
. . . and Johnny? . . . that day is here. The time is now,
Johnny. Won't that be a wonderful story to tell your
own little Johnny, Johnny? You can do it, Johnny. Let's
have a hug here, can't we, Johnny? Now, go up there to
that plate, Johnny, and bash it out of the park!"

Oh, wait! That wasn't a nightmare. That's what he
was usually saying during the games. My bad.

You're going to hear some great stories from this
guy. There's one he'll tell about the year when he
coached the best baseball player he ever saw, "The
Zipper," aka Ronald Raygun. "The Zipper," he'll tell
your team, "did it all. He could field, he could hit, and
he could pitch. He was a one-man team and the word

'give up' wasn't in his vocabulary." (Don't interrupt at this juncture of his story and point out that "give up" is two words, not one.) He'll continue. "I had Zip for two seasons, boys. At the start of our second season, ol' Zip got tonsillitis and missed our second game. I'd like to tell you that the Zipper came back to lead our team to victory, but that wouldn't be the truth. The truth is that ol' Zip got hold of some bad ice cream after he had his tonsils out and he never played again. He developed some kind of hives from that strawberry swirl that made him break out in pink blotches all over whenever he even got near a baseball field so his slacker parents refused to let him play anymore. The Zipper wanted to, believe me, but it just wasn't in the cards. Not with chicken-livered parents like that! But the ol' Zip still contributed! When I went over to his house to plead for his folks to let him play for the last time and they refused, the Zip called me to the side and said, 'Coach, if ever the team is down and out and it looks the blackest . . . tell 'em to win one for the Zipper.' I don't have to tell you boys I cried when he said that, do I? I hope not! I'm certainly not ashamed. In our last game, for the league championship, we were down one run, bottom of the ninth, bases loaded, and our worst hitter, Stanley 'Waterbug' Mirkin was at the plate with a 3-2 count. Can you guess what happened?"

At this point in his story, don't be a smart aleck and ruin it for him with one of your usual wisecrack answers! Like, "Ol' Waterbug struck out and started crying, maybe?" Not unless you really like playing right field! Just go kind of misty-eyed and nod furiously and pretend you're choking back tears. Act like you've got a lump the size of a small warthog in your throat. This will encourage him to go on with his story, which admittedly is really pathetic and sounds suspiciously like it may have been plagiarized. But if you don't let him get it out, he may well explode right in front of your eyes—and have you ever tried to get exploding coach goop off your uni? Let me tell you, it's not easy, and your mom won't be happy you were the cause of her having to spend long hours down in the laundry room hand washing it. Although, you *can* make points here by saying, "Gosh, Coach. Ol' Waterbug saved the day, didn't he?" This is the kind of question that just might get you that coveted shortstop position.

"Just wait," he'll say to your question, smiling gently and wisely at the innocence of your youth. "I'm coming to that." Here is where he takes a deep breath to compose himself for the really emotional bombshell he's preparing to drop. "Boys, I called time out and pulled Waterbug to the side. During that timeout, I told Waterbug the Zipper's story." (Resist the impulse here to ask if timeouts were a lot longer in those days, as by your calculations it had to take a half hour, minimum, to tell this particular story. Don't point out that it's already taken 28 minutes to tell this version and it obviously isn't over with yet. These kinds of remarks will only get points subtracted from your accum.) "When I finished, I looked Waterbug square in the eye and told him it was up to him to 'win one for the Zipper.' And he did."

At this point, somebody on your team will jump up and yell, "Waterbug hit a home run and won the game, right?"

Don't let that be you. That will get a dirty look from the coach.

"No," he'll say. "He didn't hit a home run. But . . . he did win the game." The coach will mumble something here that no one can make out.

"How?" some other foolish teammate will say. Again, don't let it be you.

"Well," Coach Intrepid will say, "he didn't hit a homer, exactly. He got hit by the next pitch. It forced a run in and we won. Let's do our laps, boys."

How to deal with this guy? Hang onto every word of his pep talks with rapt, bright-eyed attention (a little tear or two doesn't hurt a bit, believe me!), and when he's done and it's time to take your place in right field, let out a tremendous roar and run as hard as you can . . . into the dugout wall. Try to knock yourself out if possible. When you come to, you're going to get a pleasant surprise. He's switched you to shortstop!

You'll be a bit woozy and disoriented, but just try to get through the inning and hope no one hits it to you. If they do, try to catch the middle one of the three balls you see coming toward you. That's probably the real one. Let's hope so.

If you can run into enough walls during the season and show Coach your tremendous esprit de corps, you will be the permanent shortstop and even get to pitch now and then.

If you can't knock yourself out, at least try to smack the wall in such a way as to draw some blood. Smear it around so it looks like there's more and you can even mumble something like "I see the Light. There's a nice Woman standing there, glowing kind of yellowish."

Just don't overact.

THE "RULE BOOK" COACH

Usually also The Blusterer kind of coach.

This guy knows the rule book forwards, backwards, sideways, and inside out and always wanted to be a lawyer . . . only he couldn't get into law school. He tried, but graduating at the bottom of his high school class was a drawback. In fact, the only book he's ever mastered is . . . you guessed it . . . the Official Baseball Rules Book.

Prepare for long games. He likes to argue. With the umps, with the opposing coaches, with the fans. If he can't find anybody to argue with, he'll argue with himself. A worthy opponent if ever one lived. Over in the corner of the dugout he'll be yelling at the air and punching himself when he can't find anyone else to engage him in debate. Sometimes, when his arguing reaches its zenith, he'll take his spikes off and face them and begin kicking dirt on them. It's just his way of practicing for umpires.

He's the only one on the field who understands the infield fly rule. He loves this rule! Mostly because he's the only one who's ever read it all the way through and doped it out. Even most of the umpires you encounter in youth baseball are fuzzy on this one. He knows this from experience and he knows if he runs onto the field when they missed the call on it, he's going to win any and all arguments. He doesn't even have to look it up. He knows it by heart. He may forget his middle daughter's birthday or exactly what month it happened to be when he got married, but he knows the infield fly rule.

If wins are important to you as a player, you're gonna love him. Every season, he wins at least two games by arguing the rules, sometimes armed with the bat he likes to carry with him when he goes out for a discussion with the other coach. The other coaches know him, and when he erupts from the dugout with his trademark bellow over some rule a player just violated, they may put up a half-hearted argument, but in the end they know he's going to win.

You can recognize him by the perpetual red blush halfway up his neck.

He's also the trick-play artist. Coach Rule Book has done exhaustive research for years and years and knows where all the loopholes in the rule book are. He's the guy who trains his players to throw down their bats when the ump cries "Ball three" and trot to first and the runner on first to jog on down to second like they both thought a walk had been issued. When the other team or umpire realizes the mistake, they call the batter back and he comes, dutifully, but the runner who's reached second stays there. Either he or the coach will explain to the ump that he just stole a base. After all, it was still a live ball, wasn't it?

How to get on his good side?

This one's fairly easy. One day, in front of the team, tell him you've been reading baseball history and that there's this old-time manager he reminds you of an awful lot. Some guy named Billy Martin who used to manage the New York Yankees.

You don't even have to know who Billy Martin was. Trust me on this. *He* does and that's all that matters. That's his spiritual godfather and the only hero he's ever had in life. If you really want to get on his good side, walk around at the first practice muttering darkly that you "sure hope this here team plays some good ol' 'Billy Ball.'" Pound your glove (hard) when you say that and offer to fight anybody on the team who wants to take you on. You won't bat third, but you'll bat leadoff and be the shortstop.

He may even want to take you out barhopping with him. Just don't tell your parents where you're going. They may object.

CHAPTER
TEN

"NOSTALGIA-FREAK" COACH

This old boy is instantly recognizable. He's got "Tinker to Evers to Chance" tattooed on his upper left bicep. If it's cold out when you meet him and he's wearing long sleeves, another reliable sign is the vanity license plate on his car, which reads: "Flduvdrms."

This is in reference to that sappy and hilarious baseball movie of the same name (spelled better) that Kevin Costner starred in and that your dad made you see. Twice. Remember? It was the first time you ever saw a grown man cry. And wondered why. The first time in your young life you realized you wouldn't mind so much if they told you you were adopted and your real dad was in Sing Sing Prison.

Coach Nostalgia Freak firmly believes this is the only movie made in the past 200 years that's worth seeing. If he ever mentions it (if he doesn't, he's not Nostalgia-Freak Coach), don't point out any of the obvious fallacies contained in it. Like how it was a bit of a stretch to believe that fans were going to drive three hours to some corn field in Iowa and pay the munificent sum of six bucks and some change to watch baseball ghosts no one could see besides Kevin Costner, when, for just a couple of bucks more, they could stay home in Chi-town and watch their beloved Cubbies (the real deal . . . kinda . . .) drop two in a doubleheader to the Phillies. The only conclusion is that the Costner character's marketing approach was aimed at the dumbest baseball fans he could identify. On second thought, maybe all they had to do was put up flyers around Waveland Avenue. . . .

And don't point out that Kevin's wife in this classic is obviously the source of all the dumb blonde jokes in history. All throughout the movie, the bank is calling hourly threatening to foreclose on the family homestead and not only is she about to lose her home, her family's income, and her husband's sanity, but also all the cards for her future pretty much spell out that her main activity for the rest of her life is going to be spent in fixing Kev's lunch bucket when he has to go to work at the aluminum siding plant in town. All this going on and what does she do? Lie on her bed in a Zen trance and mumble, over and over, "A man's gotta do what a man's gotta do. A man's gotta. . . . " If you ever meet a girl like this, whatever you do, don't marry her. Can you believe she's stealing from whatever egg money is left to finance his excursions to Fenway Park and the like? Or that Kev is portrayed as this big baseball fan but when he finally gets to Fenway á la his dream (along with his ghostly sidekick, as played by the ghostly James Earl Jones) these supposedly big baseball fans (Kev and Jimmy) leave in the seventh inning? In the seventh inning? What true baseball fan leaves in the seventh inning for cryin' out loud? Especially with Luis Tiant pitching?

Anyway. Enough. The point is, if you draw a coach who thinks "The Field of Dreams" is the holiest of all movies, you can pretty safely conclude you've got a mushbrain for a leader and that you're going to hear lots of really boring stories about old geezers who played in what looked a lot like flannel underwear.

How to have a successful season under this coach? One good way is to go to bat with your hands 8 to 10 inches apart and when he sees this and looks quizzically at you, just say, "I'm trying out that Ty Cobb thingy, Coach." He's gonna love ya!

And, if he gets it in his mind to have the entire team over to his house to watch his own video of the Costner opus, do everything in your power to not laugh at the funny parts. Hint: There are a lot of funny scenes in this movie if you haven't seen it. Try to think of something sad to keep from snickering at them. For instance, picture your pet puppy being smashed by a wayward comet. . . .

CHAPTER
ELEVEN

THE "PARENTS' MANAGER"

I t'll be near the end of the season before you learn his name, but your parents will know him quite well.

The tipoff to seeing if you've lucked out and drawn this kind of manager will be during the first practice.

The Parents' Manager coach will barely look at you for the first hour of practice. Instead, he'll be over at the side, regaling the moms and dads with his vast baseball experience. All about how he played ball for the Gobbler's Knob Community Junior College and how he would've been in the Show except for that pesky groin injury suffered in the third grade that's forever nagged him and kept him from making the pivot exactly right.

He's got lots of stories. There's one where the high school coach cut him and he got revenge by making the college team. (The aforementioned GKCJC.) He neglects to add the fact that the high school team would have ten-run-ruled the "college" team by the second inning had they ever played; the GKCJC nine in those years being made up mostly of the brass section of the school's symphony and jazz club. "Buzz," the part-time volunteer coach, coerced them into playing mostly because no one else would come out for his sorry team. Though the Parents' Manager coach tells lots of stories, he usually leaves some vital element like that out.

The good thing is that you won't have to hear his stories. He is only vaguely aware that you exist. His audience is the parents.

During the games, you will rarely see him. In case you're interested, he's the older guy over at the far side of the dugout, chatting up your mom and dad.

He's the guy who's never prepared for the games. Each inning, he'll slowly come to the realization that the other team has left the field and is patiently awaiting a pitcher to hit against and some fielders to catch the ball should it be struck. He's made coaching simple in some ways. This coach doesn't take time out of his busy schedule schmoozing parents to learn names. It's easier to just call everybody "You." That's your name for the season. Sometimes, it's "Hey, You."

The usual scene is this: You're the visitors and have batted. In a democratic fashion, you and your teammates have voted on a batting lineup. (Somebody's gotta be prepared.) Now, your third batter has made his trip to the plate and the inning is over. You and your teammates look over expectantly at the adult over by the far end, laughing and regaling all the moms and dads. You kind of know ('cause you're smart) that he's the coach. After all, he's been at most of the practices. You think. You see one of the parents poke him on the arm and as he turns to view the field it dawns on him he's supposed to do something.

He's an action guy, this coach. No indecision in this man, bucko! He turns his gaze on you and your assembled teammates. You see a note of recognition in his eyes. He moves into action. "You," he says, pointing to Jason Schmidt. "You're the pitcher. You," (this to the guy standing next to him, Billy O'Dell). "You're the catcher. Get into the gear." It continues this way until he comes up with nine players. Then, little Tommy Watson steps up with a tear in his eye, bottom lip trembling, and says, "But, Coach. You promised me last game I could pitch." He ponders this a minute and then says, "Okay. You, first pitcher. You play right. This guy's the pitcher."

He goes back to the parents. He doesn't see Jason Schmidt bawling all the way out to right. Or that there's two players standing there since he's forgot already and previously assigned Nooney Williams to the same spot about two minutes before.

He misses a lot of stuff like this. Get used to it. The good thing is that if you're a born leader, *you* can coach the team. If you're not, right field awaits. . . .

He also has a son on the team. He knows his name. Sort of. He just calls him "Son."

"Son" will begin playing shortstop until he boots so many balls even Coach Dad notices. Maybe a parent says something to him. Most likely a parent says something to him. That, he pays attention to. "Son" then goes to third base, but the coach overhears another team's coach talking the next day, saying he puts his worst fielder on third since nothing's ever hit there. That's the end of Son's third-base career. He's now a first-sacker. That also ends when he misses his thirty-third straight throw over to first. It wasn't the thirty-three missed throws that got him moved. It was . . . you guessed it . . . something a parent mentioned.

There's only one place Son can never play. The outfield. Especially right field, even though it's the position he's genetically best suited for. No, he gets assigned the one position no one else will play. Yep. Catcher.

Overnight, Coach Dad is raving about Son and his expertise behind the plate. "Yeah, tough kid, just like his old man," you overhear him telling the parents. "That's the position I played." (Funny, you thought you overheard him telling the parents at that first practice he was a shortstop. . . .) You hear him telling Son one day, "Yeah, Son. Being a catcher is the quickest way to the majors. . . ."

Ah. . . . Could that be his purpose in coaching?

Don't be cynical, young man. It's not becoming.

THE "MOM" COACH

This coach usually has longer hair than the other coach-types . . . although, not always. She will have a higher-pitched voice than the other coach-types also . . . but not always. If she has longer hair and a higher-pitched voice, you're probably in good shape. If her voice sounds like a 35-year-old Mack truck grinding gears and she's wearing a stylish and precision-cut flat-top . . . try to get a transfer to another team. Unless, of course, you really enjoy whipping down the ol' pushup/wind-sprint trail. . . .

In reality, Coach Mom can be a version of any of the other coaches. Just because she's a woman doesn't mean she'll be any worse or any better than her male counterparts. In truth, she may be a better coach, as she may not know as much about baseball. How does that make her better? Simple. The first rule of coaching kids is "Do No Harm." Well, at least it *should* be. The simple fact is that many coaches *over* coach, usually with the wrong techniques, and chances are Coach Mom won't be as guilty of that.

Her son will be on the team. He will be the kid in right field. Coach Mom knows not many balls are hit there and he'll be safe as long as she can keep him there. Although . . . he may honestly belong there having earned the right by his ability. You can also tell her son since he's the one with the knee pads, the elbow pads, the mouthpiece, the heart protector, and the way he tries to change his appearance so's his teammates can't tell he's related to the coach.

His name seems to be "Sweetie . . . Oops! I Mean Bryan."

He will have a hoarse voice. His voice is a result of his many hours arguing late into the night with his mother to "please, please, please Mom—don't coach my team. I'll do anything if you just won't coach my team. I'll give up my allowance, my birthday party, that trip to Disneyland if you . . . just . . . won't . . . coach . . . my . . . team!" (That last is always delivered with a strangled cry, the same kind of sound a rabbit makes when a hawk snags him and starts to carry him away for supper for all the little hawkettes back at the nest.)

Poor guy! You gotta feel sorry for him. Just imagine what it would be like if *your* mom walked in the door one day with a baseball scorebook under her arm and asked you, "Now what does this darned 'E-6' mean? Why can't you just write little notes on the page for what players did?"

Want to play shortstop for Coach Mom? Easy. Just make enemies with her son and make sure she knows it. She knows lots of grounders are hit to short and the chances are high you'll get hit with one eventually. Of course, this can backfire on you and you may end up being the catcher. She's already had a gander at the equipment the catcher has to wear, and, being a reasonably intelligent person, has assumed that means this is a dangerous position. The perfect place to put *you*, the monster who's been unmercifully teasing her little Sweetie . . . Oops! I Mean Bryan.

She may not be your coach for long. She may possibly be coaching because Sweetie . . . Oops! I Mean Bryan's dad and her may be on the quits and he was supposed to have been the coach, but, well . . . he's ridden off to New Orleans with his new friend Trixie on the back of his new Harley Sportster and Coach Mom feels a duty not to let her baby boy down. Her ex may come back into town along about the third game, being as his new friend Trixie met another new friend down there in the Big Easy and he's back to see how Mom and Sweetie, Oops! I Mean Bryan are doing. When he arrives at the ballpark and sees Coach Mom being all warm and fuzzy with her assistant coach (the next-door neighbor whom he'd been suspicious of long before the

New Orleans trip) as they pore together over the batting order, the fur may be about to fly. If that happens, expect a new coach.

One good thing will happen in that event. Sweetie . . . Oops! I Mean Bryan, will go from being that to just plain old Bryan, and once the pressure is off him, will probably turn out to be a really neat kid. As soon as Mom is out of the coaching picture, all his pads will turn up missing and he'll be arguing with the new coach to play shortstop just like everyone else.

THE "MANIAC" COACH

The logo on this guy's shirt shouldn't be a pair of crossed bats or a smiley-face baseball, but the Looney Tunes' Tasmanian Devil cartoon. He *is* a Looney Tune!

Ever seen those photos of astronauts training for deep space? When they're in the G-force training module? The flesh and skin of their faces contorted into a horrible caricature of Attila the Hun as he might look after scarfing down sixteen chocolate bars (serious sugar rush) and running late for a massacre because his wife made him stop and do the dishes?

Whelp, thas' your Coach Maniac.

He's a doozy, fellas. You're gonna get permanent hearing damage with this guy. You've surely noticed his normal tone of voice is a scream.

He screams at everything. After awhile, you'll begin to learn his scream nuances.

"Are you insane or just vision-impaired, Clancy? That ball was thirty-five feet over your head! Shaquille O'Neal couldn't reach that one with a nine-foot bat!" This is actually his gentle way of reminding you not to swing at high ones—that if the catcher couldn't leap high enough to catch the pitch, you probably shouldn't have taken a cut at it. This is relatively mild.

He might screech something like, "Hoolihansky, you total imbecile! You didn't tag up! You didn't tag up! You didn't tag up! That was the most harebrained, moronic, stupid, thoughtless stunt you've ever pulled! You bet on the other team or something? Your dad the coach in the other dugout over there? You are a nightmare, Hoolihansky! You are a malignant tumor!" If he runs out onto the field wielding a bat in one hand while screaming this and blood is frothing in little bubbles at the corners of his mouth, this is a *serious* scream. Be afraid. Be *very* afraid. If you don't see any blood, but his voice sounds as if his vocal cords are being strangulated and ripped from their roots, this is the time to consider hopping a freight train and getting far, far away from the town he resides in. Do it now. Just run like the wind away from the direction of that terrible voice. Years later, when you return to your hometown a grown man and CEO of Oreo Cookies, Inc., you'll visit him in the insane asylum and talk to him through the little bars in the window. You'll need to do that to exorcise the demon from the past that's appeared in your dreams every night since Little League. Once you see that he's securely restrained in his straitjacket, you'll be able to get a good night's sleep. Of course, I'd still recommend you buy a police scanner, and if you hear of a breakout from the funny farm, it might be wise to "hit the mattresses"—as they say in the Mob—until you learn who's escaped.

This guy is angry at something. At first, it seems like it's just you, but that's probably not so. If you notice, I bet he yells at all of your teammates, too. His problem is, he's a perfectionist. He could never achieve perfection in his own baseball career as the substitute right fielder, but he's gonna get it with you guys.

His wife is the lady with the hangdog expression who never looks anyone in the eyes and is wearing the twin Supersonic Hearing Aids that kind of make her look like Princess Leia in "Star Wars" in silhouette. Instead of the Princess's hairdo, she's got plastic blobs on the side of her head, the aforementioned Supersonic Hearing Aids. You don't think he only yells on the baseball field, do you? Can you imagine what her life must be like when she burns the Tater Tots? She's skinny as a garter snake emerging from winter hibernation from doing laps for her various infractions.

His kid is your shortstop. Not only because he's the coach's son, but because he never ever ever makes an error. He doesn't dare make an error! He knows what will happen if he does. He's on the slim side himself. If you could visit Coach Maniac's house, you'd see a worn, circular path all around it where Mom and Junior take their daily punishment. All the windows have tiny spidery cracks from the sonic booms his voice has produced.

The best way to coexist with this coach? Read up on Zen; take a class in it if you can. Learn to find that "quiet place" deep inside when you're the target of his wrath.

If you can't do that, then inquire discretely of his wife where she purchased her hearing aids and see if she can't get you a discount. The "secret" of hearing aids (which she knows) is that you can also turn them off and not hear a blessed sound.

That's the first thing to look for. The "Off" button. And then . . . there's always that freight train. . . .

FOURTEEN

THE "PERFECT" COACH

This guy looks a lot like me. Actually, he looks *exactly* like me! If this coach appears regularly at your breakfast table, your name is Mike, your mom's name is Mary, you have two sisters named Britney and Sienna, and you pitch and play shortstop or first base on your team, the odds are really good this is your coach.

If you find yourself on this guy's team, thank your lucky stars. For some reason—probably as a reward for living a good and righteous life and getting all A's on your report cards and never once sassing your sainted mom—you have been blessed with this man for a coach. Try to be humble about your good fortune.

Repay Fortune's charity to you by being kind to others. Help little old ladies across the street when you can; do a good deed every day of your life. Don't tease any girls (with the possible exception of the really obnoxious ones).

This coach will have the infinite patience of your grandpa, the wisdom of Harry Potter, the humor of Walt Disney, the kindness of Doug on Nickelodeon. In short, he will have the personality traits of most of the coaches in the Matt Christopher baseball books (the nice ones).

His voice will remind you of the soothing sounds of a murmuring mountain stream on a clear, sunny day. Never will he raise it. He will gently point out any mistakes you might make (always in private and never in front of anyone else), and will show you instantly how to make the play the right way. In fact, everyone on his team will be so baseball-savvy and become so skilled through his tutelage that each and every one of you will eventually make it to the "Show," receiving sizeable bonuses upon signing. Enough to buy your mom and dad a new house near Disneyland and get a new Sony Playstation for yourself. At some point in the future, nearly half the major league teams will be composed of boys who played for him. The other half will wish they had.

Don't worry about having to do laps for this guy. "Laps" to him are simply those things people make when they sit down.

When you're in high school and required to write an essay titled, "The Most Influential Person in My Life," he will be your subject.

Practices are the most fun you've ever had. When your folks announce you're all going to Six Flags in two weeks, you'll beg off since that means you'll miss those great practices.

Your team will be so well prepared that you'll ten-run-rule all the other teams in your league by the second inning. Everyone's batting average will be at least .750 and by the end of the year, every single teammate (including you) will have thrown at least one no-hitter. Other kids will be crying to be on your team, to play for such a great coach, but, alas, they will have to abide by the league's roster limits. You feel a huge sadness for those poor, unlucky stiffs.

Your coach will be the only baseball man ever to win the Nobel Peace Prize and Hollywood will make a movie about him, starring Kevin Costner and some drop-dead, gorgeous actress who will be called "Mary" in the film. (His name will be "Les.") They'll have a son named "Mike" who will cut down the ash tree in their backyard and carve his bat out of it and with that bat, Mike will hit the home run in the final scene that wins The Big Ball Game (against terrible odds). It will be a strong, true, *accurate* baseball movie, unlike that "Field of Dreams" baloney.

The only reason you don't beg for him to adopt you is that you kind of like your own dad and don't want to hurt that man's feelings. (You see, you've learned Compassion from this coach.)

Even more than baseball, you will have learned about life from this man. Never will you forget the way your heart beat fast every time Perfect Coach led the team in chanting his Basic Pair O' Precepts for a Happy Life.

Remember?

They went like this: *(1) Never play poker with anyone named after a city, and; (2) Never go out with a girl named after a day of the week.*

You have a lot to be grateful to this man for, but more than anything else you have him to thank for your philosophy of life and that shining credo you learned at his feet. The best way to repay all he's done for you is to emulate his example by remaining humble and perfect for the rest of your life.

(Disclaimer) *In every other chapter in this book, the reader may discern a hint of sarcasm or irony. Not so in this chapter. Every word in this chapter is accurate and true and has been attested to and verified by a licensed notary public as to its verity.*

Your Teammates

The following section describes some of the other kids you will find on your team. It may even describe you! (Let's hope not. . . .)

THE COACH'S SON

One of the kids on your team is the coach's son. You'll be able to tell this player easily. He's the kid the coach sends out to play shortstop. He also looks a lot like the coach, only shorter and with less gray in his hair.

He's also the guy lugging the big equipment bag out to your first practice.

This might be you.

If you find yourself on shortstop in the first game, check and see if your dad's coaching the team. Chances are, he is. If you find yourself also batting cleanup, it's almost certain he is. If you're also pitching for a portion of the game, there's no doubt.

If you find yourself in this position, there's no need to read any of the following chapters on teammates.

All you need to know is that those other guys on the team are there to be your supporting cast and assist you in your quest for stardom. They may be nice guys and all, but they're woefully underprepared to play critical fielding positions like short. They failed miserably in The First and Most Important Requirement of Playing Short:

Selecting the right dad.

If, however, you're not blessed by being related to the coach in some significant way, you'll be relieved to know that you won't be required to play that nasty shortstop position.

On the other hand, if you find yourself trotting out to right field, you can be fairly sure your dad isn't the coach. Although, in that case, your mom might be. . . . An important clue here will be if the coach calls you "Sweetie, Oops! I Mean Bryan."

If you're not the coach's son and find yourself harboring hopeless dreams of playing shortstop, somebody needs to give you a crisp slap to the cranial region. What we like to call a "reality-check." You might, however, have an outside chance of playing one of the other infield positions. For tips on how to accomplish that, see chapter three, Manager-Dad. To implement your plan, and for starters, you'll need to scrounge up a ride over to your team's shortstop's house.

It helps if you realize that first base is kind of a cool position. . . .

CHAPTER
SIXTEEN

THE ALIBI-ARTIST

Y ou'll be lucky if you only have one of these on your team. This guy has an excuse for everything.

Struck out? The umpire was blind, he'll say. And probably related to the pitcher. I'm pretty sure I smelled beer on his breath. . . .

Missed that grounder? The Alibi-Artist will claim a bad hop. But . . . it was a slow roller, you point out. Yeah, he'll say; but did you see where it hit that clump of dirt and veered to the right at the last second?

Don't argue with him. You'll lose.

The Alibi-Artist has even prepared a courtroom defense *before* his appearance on the field. "That sun," he'll mutter darkly, just before he takes his spot in left field. "Nobody's going to catch a fly in left today." "But," you argue, "it's drizzling. And if the sun *was* out, it'd be behind you." "Maybe so," he'll come back with, "but have you noticed the wind? It's blowing something fierce." Not where you're standing, where it's that eerie "calm before the storm" you've read about, but don't point that out. He's already got a contingency alibi ready for that. "I didn't mean down here, dummy. Up there [pointing] where the fly balls go. You never studied aeronautics or wind currents? Twenty feet above sea level is where they always start." Or, "I missed my eye checkup appointment last Wednesday," he'll say next. "If I drop a high pop-up, blame my slacker dad for forgetting to take me. I'm probably horribly nearsighted. Is that you, Mike? It sounds like your voice."

When he wanders off first base and gets picked off, he'll return to the dugout and claim he "just had a 'senior moment'" and he hates his grandfather for passing on the affliction. "What's that?" you (foolishly) ask—"What's a 'senior moment'?"—and he'll sneer openly at your naïve question. "Gosh, does *everybody* from your class ride the short bus? A 'senior moment' is that deal where old people forget things. I come by it naturally. Genetics. My grandpop has 'em all the time." When you point out that you understand the concept, but you always thought you had to be older than nine to experience it, he'll whip out that sneer again and say, "Shows how much you know about genetics. Read a book sometime, learn something. You go to one'a them public schools or somethin'?"

When he's playing second and actually catches a grounder, but then throws the ball twelve feet over the first sacker's head, while all the runners are scampering merrily around the bases, he'll throw his glove on the ground, kick it, give himself a forearm shiver, and scream, "I told Mom not to forget my Ritalin! I don't believe that woman! Never trust anyone over fifteen!"

The trick to dealing with this guy is to simply ignore him. Never, upon any circumstance, point out the flaws in his reasoning. He is much more practiced than you'll ever be at the fine art of point-counterpoint.

Failing that (ignoring him), try to be nice to him when you're forced into personal contact.

After all, he's on the fast track to becoming a barrister of note, and there may come a day in the not-so-distant future when you'll need that brilliant legal mind which was finely tuned on the playing fields of Little League.

Like, say, when you're an adult, coaching your own team, and you throttle the little Alibi-Master who claims a sudden dust storm caused him to miss the take sign and swing at a pitch that bounced twice before it reached home plate.

Then you'll be glad you befriended this guy. He'll be the legal beagle on your defense team who comes up with the "My client was suddenly and savagely possessed with a demon spirit" defense, that springs you from the electric chair into the cushy, palatial insane asylum digs instead.

See the future and treat this guy with respect.

Make friends with him and he can even help you in your own life. You can bet that if you ask him, he will come up with a much better excuse for you than "the dog ate my homework," should the teacher inquire about your missing book report on "The Life Cycle of North American Clams."

Treat this guy as a valuable resource.

CHAPTER
SEVENTEEN

THE PEST

This is the kid who everybody fights to get away from in drill lines. When he isn't throwing clumps of dirt or pebbles at his teammates, he's giving the guy ahead of him a wedgie and screaming with shrill laughter at his moronic stunt. He's in perpetual whine mode and he's got the kind of high-pitched screechy voice that can break glass at two hundred yards. He never wonders why his only friend on the team is his first cousin, a boy remarkably like himself, right down to being a mouth-breather. Genetics? Family social environment? Who knows? Whatever caused his behavior problem seems rooted in his family structure somehow. You can see that in his loud, overbearing father, that nice man who keeps yelling insults at him during practices and games. Things like, "Get closer to the plate, sissy." This is just his somewhat peculiar way of communicating with his beloved son.

He's the inept player who's always screaming at others' mistakes, never aware that he makes fifteen errors to their one. He likes to call teammates crude names on a regular basis and has an uncanny ability to pick up on their slightest infirmities and coin a special term for each individual, the root of which lies in their physical blemish. He is certainly accomplished at doing this, having learned his vocabulary from his peers back at the trailer park. This lexicon of terms includes such endearing epithets as "Dummy," "Fatso," and "Loser." He is especially fond of the nickname "Loser" and will never think to apply the name to the appropriate time and place: namely, during his adult stage of life and on the namecard affixed to his polyester lapel he's required to wear to his annual peripheral bathroom fixtures subcontractor's annual convention and social soiree.

You've heard the term "Political Correctness?" This guy's pretty much why the movement started.

During actual games, he sometimes goes into a catatonic state in which he stares blankly at the beautiful dandelions in right field spread delightfully about him, blissfully unaware of the baseball hurtling toward him and about to land wickedly between his eyes, effectively poleaxing him and bringing him back to a conscious and alert state of being. Helping him regain that awareness will be the booming voice of Dad erupting from the stands, advising him that, "Real ballplayers don't cry," something Dad got from one of those sappy movies he likes to watch.

Whenever you hear the coach yelling, "You guys settle down in the dugout," you can be sure that he's at the center of the commotion. He's the one with the sense of humor permanently arrested at about the third grade. His intelligence seems to have been suspended at the same time.

Just look for the kid with the blank stare who breathes mostly through his mouth. When you ask him what he's thinking, he'll say, "Nothing."

He's not lying.

The best way to deal with him is to just avoid him. Especially in drill lines.

THE HOME-RUN KING

That big, beefy kid who mumbles a lot? Stands roughly 6 foot 3 inches in his spikes and blocks out the sun when you're within ten feet of him? He's your team's home run hitter and will bat cleanup.

His problem is, he usually doesn't have much of a batting average and most of his homers come in late innings against the third pitcher the opponents have put in when the game is all but over. He can't actually hit against the speed the starters usually have, but he can tee off on the slow guys. That's because he's kind of slow himself. He favors a long, sweeping batting stroke—that one your dad told you never to use. (Sometimes called a "broomstick" swing.) He swings from the heels and never hits a ground ball. Flies are his game. Once in a while, one goes over the fence. About one in every 300 to 400 at-bats. The rest of the time he whiffs or pops up to the second baseman or catcher. He likes to try to hit the bottom half of the ball. At the end of the year, his stats will read like this:

"Booger" Redwood

At Bat	Hits	1B	2B	3B	HR	RBI	BB	B.A.
54	7	1		1	5	14	1	.129

He plays third base. Nothing is going to get by this guy. Not that he'll actually catch anything—he has an aversion to bending over for a grounder—but any ball hit his way has a good probability of striking his body mass and sometimes the ball will even carom off his knee over to the first baseman if it's hit hard enough.

Sometimes, the coach will stick him on first. After all, he's a big target. Just make sure you make perfect throws to him. His idea of being "cool" doesn't include lowering his body unit or appendages for throws in the dirt.

He's just about reached the highest plateau he's capable of in baseball. Next year, he moves to a higher-age league where the fences are farther and those home runs will turn into long outs.

In batting practice, everything he hits goes out. That's because the coach/pitcher is lobbing the ball in. In a real game, with a real pitcher (a shorter, younger guy *not* lobbing the ball in), you can tell him by the sudden gust of wind he creates when he swings mightily (and a half-second late) at the ball.

When the coach first spots him, his eyes will light up. Especially after he's lobbed a few in to Booger during your first batting practice and seen ol' Boog's mighty swing. It will begin to dawn on the coach (near the end of the season) that Booger also strikes out a lot.

An awful lot.

THE "KNOW-IT-ALL" KID

There's at least one on every team. If you're lucky, there will be only one. If you get more than one, consider asking your folks to move so you can get on a different team in another town. This teammate feels it his solemn duty to inform you of each and every mistake you have ever made and will ever make. As a general rule, he tries to do this in front of the coach.

He usually has a definite body shape. Short and wiry. The "short" is the important feature. He's already showing signs of what you'll learn in adulthood is a tragic affliction, referred to as the "short man's disease." It's also the reason the Ku Klux Klan is able to attract recruits. There are some individuals in life who carry the weight of a damaged ego and the only way they know to elevate their own feelings of self-worth are to tear down the achievements of those around them.

The Know-It-All won't have any obvious skills or talents himself (except in *his* mind), but this won't stop him. He believes that his mission in life is to identify others' shortcomings, occasional mistakes, and lapses in judgment. And point them out.

Loudly.

Other ways you can identify him:

1. He has the best sneer on the team.

2. He doesn't walk normally—instead, he struts everywhere, kind of like that rooster on your grandma's farm used to before you had him for last Sunday's dinner, right after Grandpa stated he'd had just about enough of his 4:30 AM crowing every blessed day of his miserable existence.

3. A bony chest, perpetually thrust out as if someone has just stuck a gun in his spine.

When he grows up, he'll own a 'Vette and take the policeman's exam seventeen times.

Failing each time.

If he somehow passes, he'll try to become a motorcycle cop.

His wife married him because she had a father just like him and has learned she needs someone in her life to point out that she can't cook a pork roast correctly.

In high school, he'll be the kid with the six dozen keys on a long chain he wears on his belt, and at recess, instead of joining the other kids in the gym for a game of b-ball, he hangs out with the janitor in the boiler room.

But for now, his only job will be to provide the thorn in your side.

A word of advice: Don't try to remove the thorn. It will only become more deeply embedded.

Even when you make a play that has a good result, like catching a fly or getting a hit, he'll find something wrong with how you did it.

"You were lucky to nail that pop-up with that Willie Mays' basket catch," he'll say of your inning-ending fielding gem. "Don't you know it's 'fingers up' on a fly?"

"It was an inch and a half from the ground when I got there," you might (foolishly) reply.

"You've got to learn to bend your knees and get low," will be his retort.

Or—"Nice triple. Why didn't you go home?"

Don't say, "Because the third baseman was holding the ball six inches from me." Why shouldn't you say that? Because, goofus. Because he'll reply, "I thought that'd be your excuse. I was pretty sure you hadn't checked out his arm and didn't know he couldn't throw hard to the catcher. If you'd known that, you'dve known you'da been safe by a mile. Plus which the catcher wasn't looking his way and would've dropped it for sure. You just cost us a sure run."

The best way to defuse this germ isn't to get up in his face or argue with him. That's playing right into his hands. It's what he wants.

Instead, agree with him.

Yes. That's right. I said *agree* with him.

Only do it *slickly*. Be smart about this, dude.

In what *seems* to be a totally straightforward acknowledgment of your ineptitude, answer his criticism like this:

"You know, Spidey, you're right." (Smack yourself hard on the forehead at this point with the palm of your hand.) "I am a complete doofus and horrible misfit on this here team, Spide. There's no reason I shouldn't have snagged that line drive, even if it was seven and a half feet over my head. If only I woulda jumped higher!" (Smack yourself *really* hard in the forehead here.) "If I'd only used your own incredible jumping technique, I would have caught that darned ball. Spidey, I wish I had even a tenth of your extraordinary Superman-like ability, because if I did, there wouldn't be a runner standing on third just now. I curse the day I was born me and not you. I only wish you could play all nine positions at once and then I could just sit in the dugout and admire you from afar like everyone else. Spidey, if I stay after the game, would you be willing to linger with me and show me how to make that play? I know I will never approach your genius with this ol' game o' rounders, but maybe I could become a tenth as good, and I'd be deliriously happy with that. And, Spidey? Do you happen to have a photo of yourself I could have? I want to pin it up in my bedroom, right between the posters of Ken Griffey Jr. and Barry Bonds. You belong up there with those guys. I see you as someday being on the same All-Star team they are. Indeed, I am already puzzled as to why the Hall of Fame committee hasn't been in contact with you, asking for the bat you hit that single with—you know, the single you got three games ago—to place on display in Cooperstown. Spidey, do I have to tell you you're my hero? I hope it's obvious you are. Someday, I only hope to be half as good as you are. Even though in my heart of hearts I know that to be an impossible dream and far beyond my humble abilities."

Just keep talking like this until he walks away. He will. Probably to the laughter of your teammates, whom he's undoubtedly chastized in the past as well. Also, probably muttering to himself, shaking his head in disgust, and kicking at the dirt.

This strategy takes a couple of times to work. He'll jump on your next mistake, same as always. Just begin the same kind of spiel. Agree with him. *Over*agree with him. He'll walk away again and probably quicker this time. For an especially persistent Know-It-All, it will maybe take three or four times of doing this, but trust me—eventually, he'll quit remarking on your errors.

He'll just find someone else to pick on. If that boy has been lucky enough to read this book and knows the strategy as well and employs it, he'll be off to another teammate until he finds the poor soul who hasn't read this. If you're smart, you'll share the wisdom you've found here with all your teammates and this guy will be toast.

Unless, of course, he's also the coach's son. . . .

In that case, I'd talk to Dad and ask if his company might have any possible openings in another town he finds attractive. . . .

THE "FISH-OUT-OF-WATER"

This is the teammate who is clearly out of his element. From the first day of practice, it's obvious he doesn't understand or even like the game of baseball. He's utterly lost no matter where the coach puts him. If you're wondering why he's even playing, look over at the stands and find the taller version of him. That's his dad and the only reason Fish-Out-of-Water is on the field. If he had his druthers, he'd probably be reading a good book in the hammock in his backyard.

Be kind to this guy. It's not his fault.

He's only out here to please his papa.

Away from the diamond, he's one of the nicest guys you'll ever meet.

Eventually, it will become painfully clear even to his father that he doesn't belong out there with a glove stuck on his hand (possibly the wrong one!) and that will be the end of his career. If he's lucky, he may have a mom with some smarts and he'll be allowed to end his baseball days even sooner.

But for now you're stuck with him.

Count on "The Fish" to come to bat with the game on the line. You know—that time in the contest when your team has just rallied back from a 9-0 deficit with eight runs in the bottom of the seventh. The bases are loaded, there are two outs, and he's at bat. (He always bats last in the order. Unless he's the coach's son. . . .) All he has to do is draw a walk or get hit by the pitch, and you tie the game. More importantly, the top of the order comes up if he can just get on base. However . . . you know better than to count on a hit by this guy. He's never actually struck the ball in his life. That's kind of hard to do when your swing always comes 4.5 seconds after the pitch has settled into the catcher's glove. Closing your eyes and bailing out toward third doesn't help either.

Expecting him to hit the ball is pointless—it just ain't gonna happen. Tell your teammates to start getting lined up to congratulate the other team. It's just about time to collect your treat ticket from the Team Mom and listen to the coach give you the Cubs's mantra in his postgame remarks.

Wait'll next game. We'll get 'em then.

Help this guy out all you can with tips and advice on how to survive the hot corner should the coach stick him there some inning. After all, except for the luck of the parent-draw, this could be you!

If you're tempted to say something cruel, always remember that it's not his fault he's on the team.

THE "KISS-UP"

Y ou've met this kid. If you haven't, you will. He's the one with the invisible umbilical cord attached to the coach. If he gets beyond its fifteen-foot length and severs it, he loses his life support and turns into his natural alien form. A blob of jelly.

When the coach has the team gather 'round him on the grass for a skull session, look for The Kiss-Up at the very front. He's the one whose arm is always stuck high in the air and waving furiously whenever the coach asks a baseball question. For that matter, *any* question. Just look for the waving arm and underneath it will be The Kiss-Up.

He has appointed himself the coach's eyes on the field, or, as you may prefer to refer to him, the "Team

Snitch." You'll hear his strident voice constantly, and somewhere in what he's babbling in his sing-song voice, your name will be floating around. As: "Hey, Coach! Johnny's screwing around in the dugout." (As are eleven others. . . .) Or, "Hey, Coach! Look out there in right field. Johnny's just standing there. He's not in the 'ready' position you told us to be in last Thursday. My gosh! He's not even looking toward home plate!" (Doesn't matter that the game hasn't actually begun and that there's no batter at the plate yet.)

He's actually a pretty smart cookie. He's realized he's not going to go all that far with his own limited baseball talent and knows the shortest route to that prized short-stop position is through sucking up to the coach. And that's best accomplished by pointing out everyone else's mistakes and horrible, antisocial behavior.

And, if he's also the coach's son, you're in for ten times the misery. He has all that downtime between practices and the games to really lay the pipe in his mission of spelling out in detail all his teammate's faults to Coach Dad.

How to deal with him? Well, murder's probably illegal in your state, so cross that off your list of possible strategies. Besides, even if it wasn't (illegal), an offense like that wouldn't look all that great on your resume when it comes time to leave home and enter that "real world" your folks keep yapping about. (Like, what are you in now if not the "real world"? Fantasy Island?)

No, the best way to deal with The Kiss-Up is to turn the tables on him. When he advises the coach that "Johnny made a face when you told us to take a lap," don't scowl at him and invite him (under your breath) to meet you under the stands after practice. No, smile pleasantly, and say something like this: "Thank you, Stanley, for pointing out my rude behavior. Stanley, I'm happy you've introduced this session and are showing us how confrontational therapy works to rid us of all those irritating neuroses we all seem to have. It's my turn, right? For helping me see my own problems, Stanley, I want to return the favor and do my part in keeping this group therapy puppy moving. First, did you know you have a bad habit of picking your nose when the other team has a runner on? That part isn't so bad, but what I'd focus on is eliminating your follow-up habit of snarfing it down. I think that's why you made that bad throw to first in the last game. Correct me if I'm wrong, but wasn't the ball slathered with green mucus, perhaps causing it to slip on your errant toss?"

A couple of similar remarks, of course uttered with only the purest of motives—to return Stanley's helpful comments designed to correct your own behavior—will do much more to curtail his own comportment than it would if you simply said, "Stuff a sock in it, Stanley."

If the coach laughs, you've won.

If he doesn't . . . right field awaits.

CHAPTER TWENTY-TWO

THE "SPACE CADET"

He's the gardener of the team. Remember back in your t-ball days? That kid in right field who was always sitting down, plucking dandelions, and blissfully ignoring the fly ball speeding his way?

He hasn't changed. He still patrols the right field garden. After six years of baseball, it's almost the way he likes it. The dandelions have all been picked and he's nearly rid the area of all the rocks and stones.

He's also an aviation enthusiast. Hope like crazy that a ball isn't hit his way whilst an airplane is droning 'cross the friendly skies. That's where his attention will be fixed. Unless, of course, a butterfly flutters across his field of vision. Butterflies trump airplanes with him. Butterflies are just plain riveting to this fellow. He lives for Monarch sightings.

When your team is up to bat and the coach goes berserk, yelling, "Where in the heck is our on-deck guy? Who's up next?" look for the kid over in the corner holding his baseball glove over his Game Boy to hide it. That's your on-deck batter.

He could also be your President some day. If he is, thank the stars he isn't in charge of anything important in your life. Like the guy who writes out and signs the paychecks for the company you'll work for. When you become an adult, try not to work for a company located near an airport or with nearby fields that are attractive to butterflies—it'll probably attract dudes like this.

He'll lead the team in one important statistic. "POB." (That stands for "Picked Off Base" in case you didn't know.) He refuses to let a minor thing like a baseball game get in the way of an important daydream, and *always* gets picked off. Usually, to end a rally.

What to do about this guy? Well, electric shock therapy works in some cases. A cattle prod applied to the buttocks at the right moment does wonders to promote alertness. If, however, professional cattle ranch instruments aren't readily accessible at your local mall, you might consider tricking him at opportune and timely moments. Like when a fly ball is whizzing toward him in right field, yell out loudly, "Clarence! Look at the big white round moth comin' atcha! If you catch it, you can mount it for your collection!" Or, if by some miracle he got on base (probably got hit by the pitch as he was concentrating on what he had for breakfast two days ago), you can scream, "Stay on the heliopad, Clarence! You're not cleared for takeoff!" Take advantage of his interest in nature and avionics.

Okay. So my "solutions" aren't perfect. You got any better ideas? If you come up with a better one, let his teachers in on it. Especially if he's in your class. Help them out and I guarantee an A for you.

CHAPTER
TWENTY-THREE

LOUD, OBNOXIOUS KID

ou don't need any help figuring out who this guy is, do you? If you can't, check out your mirror. It may be you. Every team has one, so if you can't deduce who it is . . . well. . . .

One thing's for sure—*Librarian* isn't on his list of career possibilities, even though he'd be a natural at the gig. He's heard "shhhh" and "shut up!" enough times to be able to enunciate it properly to others.

He can also do everything better than you can. If you doubt this, just ask him.

He comes in all body styles. You'd think he'd be a big round voicebox in a baseball jersey and pants, but not necessarily. He can be that short squinty guy who always runs out to shortstop. In fact, he probably is. He might also look a lot like that weird kid actor with the glasses who's in all those G-rated movies. You know—the movie star kid all the girls in your class think is "cute" and who, if he lived in your house, you'd push down the basement stairs. Every day. Or at least take his lunch money. The only physical trait that Loud, Obnoxious Kid shares with his Co-Obnoxiates is his voice. That's right—it's loud and obnoxious. Duh!

That voice will wake you at midnight. It will appear in your nightmares on a regular basis. You'll lie awake, drenched in sweat, not daring to go back to sleep for fear he'll reappear.

He's the Monster in Your Closet, the Ogre Under the Bed. He's come to life and is on your team. He has a face now. And a name. It's "Boomer." That's what the coach has nicknamed him. Coach thinks Boomer is a holler guy and he needs him on the team. He is. A holler guy, that is. You disagree with the coach about how much the team needs him.

He does serve one useful purpose. Later in life, when you become a teenager, you may decide to go to some rock concerts. Having experienced Boomer, you'll be well prepared. Those giant amps cranking out fifty million decibels that are shattering your friends' ears? The noise'll be like a whisper to you. Your eardrums will have already been shattered a long time ago.

The best way to handle him is to feed him. Always carry sacks of popcorn and keep handing him a new bag as soon as he finishes the last one. It won't keep him from screeching around the dugout, but the popcorn will muffle his voice somewhat, and, with a little bit of imagination, you can pretend it's not him you're hearing, but the roar of Niagara Falls.

If that doesn't work, get your buds together, pin him down, and put a dog muzzle on him.

Don't let the coach catch you doing this. He won't understand why you're silencing his holler guy.

Especially if it's his son.

CHAPTER TWENTY-FOUR

THE SUPERSTAR

Yeah. Your team has to have one. Mr. Perfect. Don't you just hate him? He never drops a fly, the grounder doesn't live that can hop over *his* glove at the last second, and he actually makes that awful puce and green uniform your team has been issued look good. Dude! How does he do that? You keep tripping over your own extra-extra-large shirttails that trail on the ground and his uni looks like it was tailored specifically for him.

Don't even mention his batting average. Currently, he's hitting .850, a new league record. Beating last year's record . . . which he also owns. The lowest he's ever hit in a season was .550, and that was the summer he broke his arm in three places and had tuberculosis. They let him out of the T.B. sanitarium for the games and he had to bat with one hand only, which is why he had such an abysmal B.A. that year (for him). Plus, not to mention, he also had a sty in one eye and wore a patch over it. Did I neglect to say he broke his arm diving over the fence for what should have been a homer, said catch winning the game? And caught it in deep center field, running to make the play from his shortstop position?

Baseball season for him lasts twelve months. He's enrolled at that pricey baseball school and has three ex-major leaguers tutoring him on such things as "Developing the Wheel Play" and "How to Conduct an Interview after a Four-Homer Day and Appear Humble to the Media."

His dad has built him a batting cage in the backyard . . . just to the left of the full-size baseball diamond he's also laid out, complete with dugouts and an exploding scoreboard. You were in his house once and got a gander at his trophy room and the six dozen tastefully displayed assortments of medals, championship banners, retired jerseys, award ribbons, and first-place cups he's been busy accumulating. While you were there, he got a collect phone call from Barry Bonds, who wanted some advice on why he was suddenly hitting fly balls to the second baseman instead of shots to McCovey Cove.

You overheard your dad late one night, begging your mom to consider adopting him in the event Superstar's own parents got erased in some horrible automobile accident.

He spends his time between innings at the sideline fence signing autographs for little kids. And for the umpires.

After the game, there's always a dozen or so eleven-year-old female "groupies" waiting for the coach to be done with his post-game remarks so's they can take him over to the concession stand and buy him a slushie. Each.

You know what that group of grizzled-looking old men in wrinkled Hawaiian shirts huddled together in a corner of the grandstands is. They're scouts from all the major league teams. You know they're not here to look at you. They're there to check out the kid who throws 97 mph but still isn't quite tall enough to ride the adult rollercoasters. You-Know-Who.

When he smiles, you hear a distinct "*ting!*" and are momentarily blinded by the dazzle.

When he hits, he shatters the bat. The *aluminum* bat.

Not only is he a switch-hitter, he can also throw and catch with either hand. Equally well.

You look out at the field when he approaches the plate with the bat in his Mark McGuire-sized mitts and notice all the opposing outfielders have positioned themselves on the *other* side of the fence. Approximately twenty yards behind it. The third baseman is now in left field, and guess where the first baseman is. The pitcher has picked up the rubber and placed it where second base used to be. Your opponent's shortstop and second basemen have refused to take the field. Their catcher hasn't even taken his glove out with him to his position. He knows the pitch will never get to him. He knows this because Mr. Superstar has already stretched out his arm and pointed a confident finger at center field. He's also heard the rumor that Mr. Superstar promised a home run to a dying kid in the hospital. He's actually promised a home run to four different dying kids—one per each sad and terminal—and the only thing that will stop him is if your team ten-run-rules the other team and they end the game early, before he gets his four at-bats. The only reason that probably won't happen is that none of the rest of you is any good and probably won't get on base. Most of your games end up 4-0, especially when he pitches.

What to do about this guy?

Why do anything?

He's gonna bring your team the league championship and you're all going to get a nifty trophy.

So what if he's unbearable? *You're gonna get a trophy!*

Just be sure to get his autograph for yourself. Someday you'll be able to sell it on eBay, and there's your college education, all paid for.

Get *two* autographs and you can afford Harvard.

Plus a snazzy new red sports car to drive around on campus.

Dude!

You're stylin' now.

Parents

This section deals with the kinds of parents you're likely to encounter. Yours and your teammates'. Your parent(s) will be the one(s) whose voice(s) pierces through all the others when you strike out, helping you to realize that—in case you didn't fully comprehend your mistake—you really shouldn't have swung at that pitch in the dirt.

The following chapters will help you identify the various parent species and show you how to deal with them.

(Mainly by . . . you probably saw this coming . . . arranging to not being related to them.)

A word of caution here. If you suspect your own parental unit is one of the more zeroid types outlined here, don't waste your time and energy by leaving this book where he (or she) can find it, conveniently opened to the chapter listing his traits. Trust me, he won't recognize himself.

Even if his picture is included.

It's a genetic flaw in parental DNA.

CHAPTER
TWENTY-FIVE

THE CRITIC

This is the Siskel and/or Ebert of the baseball world. His (or her: moms aren't exempt) passion in life is to review his son's performance on the diamond—before, during, and after the game. Or practice. He doesn't miss many practices. Not nearly as many as his son would like him to.

He doesn't miss many of his son's mistakes, either. More accurately, he doesn't miss *any*. He can even find some no one else can, including the coach, fellow teammates, and his son himself.

If this is your dad, when you run to the car, flushed with the rosy glow of a 3 for 4 afternoon, you're on your way to a pop exam as to why you flied out to deep center on that one at-bat.

Even when you do well, you'll discover you did badly.

"I know you caught that fly," he'll say on the (long) ride home. "But you caught it sideways. I'm *so* disappointed in you! Not fingers up. You think Ken Griffey Jr. catches flies sideways? Yeah, right. If Ken Griffey Jr. caught flies that way, he wouldn't be in the majors. On a girls' softball team, that's where he'd be. You want to end up on a girls' softball team?"

Don't reply, "Well, if the pay's good and you won't be around, then yeah, maybe. Would they be *cute* girls?" If you have to ask, "Why not?" then you haven't been paying attention here. That kind of answer will get you the same reaction from Pops that it did the time you asked for a raise in your allowance. You know, when he said, "You think money grows on trees around here?" and you answered, "Not on any in our backyard."

Don't go there. Just nod your head seriously and say, "Sir! Yessir! No excuse, sir!" This is what he wants to hear. And, for gosh sakes! Get your fingers up next time! Even if the ball's so low you have to dig a hole to get under it for that "fingers up."

Just start digging.

Look at the situation this way. It could be a lot worse. Dad could also be your coach.

Oh.

He is?

My.

Oh, my.

CHAPTER TWENTY-SIX

THE COMMENTATOR

This is the parent providing the play-by-play for the other parents' benefit. Just in case they are too dumb to understand what they're witnessing on the field, he's there to provide expert analysis.

Usually, he's a slight, wimpy kind of guy who's terrified of his boss and other adult-types in real life. But when he takes his place in the stands he is suddenly transformed into Mister Absolute Authority on Baseball.

Problem is, most of his observations come after the fact.

"I knew the left fielder should have shaded to his right," he'll say, immediately following the grounder that skipped through.

Or, "Why'd the coach let Bobby swing at that high pitch?" He probably won't stop to consider that Bobby *always* swings at high pitches and the coach hasn't figured out how to attach electrodes to Bobby's skull so that he can apply a small electric shock each time Bobby makes that mistake.

Most of his critique is directed toward the coaching boners he observes, those criticisms centered on his conviction that his own son should be playing shortstop instead of the right field area he regularly patrols. It matters not to The Commentator that his baby boy leads the team in errors and can barely lob the ball twelve feet (with a good headwind). It's the coach's fault for not giving him a chance. All the kid needs is confidence (in his eyes) and the coach has taken that away from him by sticking him in right field. If only the coach could see his kid at home in the backyard, snagging those grounders and pasting the stuffing out of the ol' whiffle ball!

The Commentator likes to recruit other parents to his way of thinking as well. Most of the time, these will be the parents of the substitute right fielder and the mom and dad of the kid who bats last in the lineup (if it isn't his kid). They are sympathetic, being as they're in the same dinghy, so to speak.

When The Commentator observes his own son is batting a lusty .043, he'll approach the coach after a game and inquire, "Don't you think you ought to spend more time on batting in practice, Coach?" The coach will be somewhat bewildered at this query, as the collective team's B.A. is .429 and would be over .600 if it wasn't for . . . guess who.

What to do about this guy? Well, radiation works for other cancers, but probably won't for this type.

I'd advise to follow your own parents' lead in dealing with this guy.

Ignore 'im.

If the "right people" observe him in his normal mode—shaking his head and mumbling beneath his breath—they'll take care of the problem. The aforementioned "right people" will be a pair of large, beefy men dressed in white uniforms. One will be armed with a big net that looks like a butterfly net on steroids, and the other will be holding out a funny-looking jacket with really long sleeves, and saying things like, "It's okay. We're here to help you, sir. We're going to take you to a nice place with central air conditioning and pretty nurses. Well . . . air conditioning, anyway. And lots of crafts. You ever macrame? You're gonna love the Chinese checkers tournaments, sir."

If these guys don't show up, your best bet is to refuse the shortstop position if it's assigned to you. That's where he thinks his son should be playing and if you get it instead, you'll hear your name a lot from the stands. Like every time you don't hit a homer or strike out the side when you're pitching.

After all, *his* kid would have.

He just needs another chance.

Maybe twenty chances. . . . Thirty?

CHAPTER TWENTY-SEVEN

THE PRACTICE "SPECTRE"

This is the parent who shows up at the first practice (and all the subsequent practices) and hangs around the sidelines.

His job is to be sure his son is treated right.

Treated "right" means he gets the shortstop spot, regardless of his ability. Failing that, Spectre Dad's next mission is to be sure his namesake isn't stuck out in right field.

He also hopes he gets asked to help out by the coaches. If this happens, he knows all will be right in heaven and on earth. Becoming a part of management assures his son won't be overlooked. Or bat ninth.

He knows. He's done this before. Every year since his son's second year in t-ball. He didn't hang around during his first year and guess what happened. That's right—his son played thirty-five feet behind the first baseman. You know where.

Ain't never gonna happen again!

Get used to his presence.

He's not going away.

If you find yourself in right field, ask your own dad what he's doing in the late afternoons. Try to persuade him to attend some of your practices.

You fight fire with fire.

In Conclusion . . .

SOME FINAL ADVICE

This book up to this point has described some of the more "extreme" types in youth baseball—coaches, fellow teammates, and parents. There are many more I haven't touched on, but you know 'em. If it seems like youth baseball represents a fairly miserable period in a young boy's (or girl's) life, that's because . . . it does! Well, not really . . . not always. It can be a really great time and the source of many fond memories. Especially if you're—you guessed it!—the coach's son. Or if you're a natural ballplayer who could throw a rising fastball while still in the crib. For some of the rest of you, it can be a somewhat frustrating part of life. Some of the doofuses you find in charge of your sports life and inhabiting your baseball universe can be really disheartening. The best defense against the real clowns is—hey, you're good!—you guessed it again! That's right—the best defense is—*humor*!

No tyrant can stand against the withering sound of laughter directed toward him.

There are also an awful lot of good guys and gals in youth baseball. There are coaches who give unstintingly of themselves and their free time and genuinely enjoy the game of baseball and the kids they're in charge of. Many of them have sons or daughters who *do* belong at shortstop and on all-star and travel teams and because of their abilities, not because of who their dad is. The truth is, most kids become good ballplayers because they've practiced more. And coach's kids, as a rule, practice more with their dads than most of the other kids do. Many times fathers become coaches because of their own son's love of baseball. Their boy has a passion for the game and it has infected the dad as well.

Be as fair in your judgment of these kids and their fathers as you'd like to be judged yourself if you were in their place. If the kid's a better player, then he should be on short. If his batting average is .500, he probably should be batting third in the lineup. In other words, if the coach is a fair person, be fair with him and respect him or her.

It's also tough to be the coach's son. His dad usually expects more out of him than he does the other players, and is often the hardest on his own boy. Also, much of the time, the parents of the other kids have a bit of a blind spot when it comes to their own kids and may see them as better players than they really are. As do coaches, sometimes. All of us as parents love our sons and daughters and want the best for them. Sometimes, we get carried away with those desires and our judgment becomes cloudy.

Don't follow our lead in that instance. Keep your own baloney detector working properly. Laugh at the jerks and respect the good guys.

I think that's what you'll do anyway, right?

If you find yourself in right field and/or batting last, ask yourself if you really deserve your fate. Be honest. If you do, accept your lot and play your hardest. Have fun with the game. And that's what it's supposed to be, you know, *a game*. If it were your job, the umpire would say, *"Work* ball!" He doesn't though. If you've noticed, he almost always yells, *"Play* ball!" If you've been unfairly treated, accept that as well. Next year's a'comin' and you'll probably have a different coach and different teammates.

Just remember that baseball's like life. It's a cycle. Goes up and down. When you're down, that usually means it's about due to swing up. When you're up . . . well, let's not talk about that.

The best take on the game of baseball was uttered by the character Ebby Calvin (Nuke) LaLoosh in the movie *Bull Durham*. If you saw the movie, you'll remember Nuke as the right-handed pitcher who didn't always know where his 98-mph fastball was going, and of whom was said by an admirer, that he "had a million-dollar arm and a five-cent head." Nuke said (accurately) that baseball was a simple game. "You throw the ball, you catch the ball, you hit the ball. Sometimes you win, sometimes you lose, sometimes it rains."

That's the game of baseball, kids, described the best I've ever heard it explained.

In closing, let me leave you with some wisdom that you can take with you and use for the rest of your life. Follow these precepts and you'll have a happy and successful life, even beyond those halcyon days of your youth. I can practically guarantee it.

Coach Les's Immutable Laws

1. *Never play poker with anyone named after a city.*

. . . and . . .

2. *Never date a girl named after a day of the week.*

And . . . always choke up and protect the plate when you have two strikes against you!

See ya in the Bigs!

(I'll be the ex-right fielder cheering you on from the cheap seats!)

ABOUT THE AUTHORS

Mike Edgerton

At this writing, Mike is a thirteen-year-old middle school student, recently graduated from the seventh grade at Blackhawk Middle School in Fort Wayne, Indiana. A star pitcher, this summer he's playing "up" for a fourteen-year-old travel team, the Frozen Ropes, who will make an appearance in the USTOC World Series later in the summer. Besides playing baseball and basketball, Mike is an honor-roll student, plays tenor sax for the school jazz band, and is a member of Blackhawk's Student Academic Team. He was selected a year ago for Northwestern University's "Gifted and Talented" Program for academically gifted middle school students. This book was his idea and most of the characters depicted were suggested and described by him. As a pitcher, he knows that you never throw a change-up to a batter having trouble catching up to his fastball, but he sometimes has trouble remembering to straighten up his room or make his bed—though he is an absolute whiz at mowing the lawn.

Les Edgerton

This is Les's seventh book in print, and his work has been nominated for a number of literary awards. His most recent book was *Finding Your Voice: How to Put Personality in Your Writing* from Writer's Digest Books. He has coached youth baseball for seven years and has an overall losing record as a coach. (But doesn't care.)